Dom Moraes (1938–2004), poet, novelist, and columnist, is seen as a foundational figure in Indian English Literature. In 1958, at the age of twenty, he won the prestigious Hawthornden Prize for his first volume of verse, *A Beginning*, going on to publish more than thirty books of prose and poetry. He was awarded the Sahitya Akademi Award for English in 1994. He has won awards for journalism and poetry in England, America, and India. He also wrote a large number of film scripts for BBC and iTV, covering various countries such as India, Israel, Cuba, and Africa.

Also by Dom Moraes

Green Is the Grass: Essays on Cricket (1951)

A Beginning: Poems (1957)

Poems (1960)

John Nobody: Poems (1965)

Mrs Gandhi: A Biography (1980)

Absences: Poems (1983)

Collected Poems: 1957–1987 (1987)

Serendip (1990)

Never at Home: An Autobiography (1992)

My Son's Father: An Autobiography (1968)

Out of God's Oven: Travels in a Fractured Land, co-authored with Sarayu Srivatsa (2002)

The Long Strider: How Thomas Coryate Walked from England to India in the Year 1613, co-authored with Sarayu Srivatsa (2003)

A Variety of Absences: The Collected Memoirs of Dom Moraes (2003)

Selected Poems, Ed. Ranjit Hoskote (2012)

Where Some Things are Remembered: Profiles and Conversations (2018)

Under Something of a Cloud: Selected Travel Writings (2019)

GONE AWAY
An Indian Journal

DOM MORAES

SPEAKING TIGER

SPEAKING TIGER BOOKS
4381/4, Ansari Road, Daryaganj
New Delhi 110002

First published in the UK by William Heinemann Ltd. UK, 1960
This edition published in India by Speaking Tiger in paperback 2020

ISBN: 978-81-944729-5-7
eISBN: 978-81-944729-6-4

10 9 8 7 6 5 4 3 2 1

Typeset in Adobe Garamond Pro by Jojy Philip, New Delhi
Printed at Chaman Enterprises, New Delhi

Contents

Introduction

Adil Jussawalla, poet and archivist extraordinaire, told me about how he had first heard of Dom Moraes in the 1950s, when both were at school, Adil at Cathedral and John Connon and Dom at St Mary's, a Jesuit institution.

'I had a friend who had also been to St Mary's who told me about this prodigy whose essays were legendary,' Jussawalla said.

I thought about this when I saw a certificate Dom had won at St Mary's (Cambridge Section) on 1 December 1951. It was for the 'The English Essay Prize'. Only, the certificate was for a scholarship; the word 'scholarship' had been scored out and 'The English Essay Prize' inserted above it. That was what the Cambridge Section of St Mary's was like at the time; that was what the city was like; that was what the country was like. It was a time of making do. And so both young men of promise left and went to England to study. They had very different experiences there with very different results.

In 1959, Dom Moraes would come back to the city of his birth to write about it and about India. He was by now a certified prodigy; he had won the Hawthornden Prize in 1958, established by Alice Warrender for a work of the imagination, to be awarded to a writer under the age of forty-one. Dom wasn't yet twenty when he won it. Other winners were Vita Sackville-West and David Garnett. The very next year Alan Sillitoe would win it for *The Loneliness of the Long-Distance Runner*; later V.S. Naipaul,

Ali Smith and Jennie Uglow would all win it. In a book of poems called *John Nobody*, published in 1965, Dom would write, 'My agent tells me that I have a name/An audience waits for what I say.'

The confidence of that line is already clear in *Gone Away*. His prose is clean and clear; his lines are shapely and elegant. His writing could be a how-to manual for the young writer (and here Speaking Tiger is owed a huge debt of gratitude for bringing us *When Some Things are Remembered* and *Under Something of a Cloud*, selections of Dom's travel writings and reportage, recently, besides reissuing his autobiographies, *My Son's Father* and *Never at Home*). But the young writer might also see that the elegance, the clarity is hard-won; and these qualities make a beautiful carapace for his discomfort. It was this divine discomfort that shaped Dom's writing. I might go as far as to say that it was what produced most of it. His poems are precise and beautifully shaped. For a man who had no time for music, they were metrically correct, just as his prose sentences played to an inner beat. Both are saved from the bloodlessness of only-beauty by the underlying inferno of emotion that is only hinted at.

It is impossible to consider what these emotions might be, so well are they camouflaged in the presentation of reality we see in *Gone Away*. (For a Rashomon moment, you might want to read Ved Mehta's *Walking the Indian Streets*, which deals with much the same moment and many of the same events but tells another story altogether.) There is in this telling as much of Dom as there is of India—he says with fetching self-irony: 'I found myself very interesting.' We would call this self-implication today, the belief that you cannot tell the story without also presenting the prism through which it is told. Dom's father was Frank Moraes, one of the greatest Indian editors ever. This must have eased Dom's path and made some contacts easier. He had only to pick up the phone for Mulk Raj Anand to suggest that he come over right away. And when he went to Delhi and got to meet Khushwant Singh, he could get drunk and conflate Beowulf and William

Blake without a care in the world because everyone would only be gently amused. (Of Singh, he says, 'He is a rich-natured Sikh, with a curious fierceness and quickness of manner, shading down to a tender understanding.' I don't know how anyone could have put it better.)

Likewise, Narayana Menon was available to give him the latest army gossip and to play the veena for his young guest, begetting an interesting description, a strange description, of a kind I have not read before or since:

> The veena is shaped like half a pumpkin on a stick. The strings are of silver, and strung crosswise across the pumpkin-face. Narayana twiddled a few keys, tautening the strings, then bent over the instrument and began to play it. The long, very flexible fingers of his left hand struck the strings slowly, and a long-drawn-out succession of notes, like the calls of a mechanical bird, filled the room. Each faded out and was imperceptibly replaced by another, or overlapped and sang at different ends of the same golden bough.

Sometimes, you get the feeling you're climbing a set of stairs. First Mulk, then Nissim Ezekiel, then Khushwant Singh, then Narayana Menon....and drumroll! Pandit Jawaharlal Nehru!

More than anything, you feel in all this the sense of a watchful alien, not unsympathetic to local life forms but not quite understanding them either. Physical unease is easy to describe: the heat, the humidity, the air-conditioning 'spreading a coolness as unhealthy as the heat', the squishy feeling under his feet at the country liquor bar; however the unease of the mind, or the spirit, is often best when it is only suggested. In each portrait in *Gone Away*, in each interview, there is a sense of mismatch. In the best traditions of journalism, Dom Moraes is not expecting something but he seems unsure whether what he does encounter is what he should be encountering. He is in free fall through India, and the only thing that will steady him is to put everything into deadpan prose. And so there is no judgement made here, and the reader can make her own decisions as she goes along.

She may choose to reject Dom-as-Virgil on the grounds that he has been colonized only too well. She may choose to look at this book as being a precursor of *India: A Wounded Civilization* in which another brilliant prose stylist, V.S. Naipaul, turned his gaze upon the enigma of this country. But she cannot claim that the author has been anything but honest in his revelations of himself.

Now that we know who this Dom is, we can tell why he is so ill-at-ease in the country of his birth. We know it is not just a matter of privilege. He has had his fair share of knocks; a peripatetic childhood in the shadow of a famous father, a mother whose mental illness left scars of all kinds, early success which can be a cross to carry, the constant feeling of disconnectedness. We know it is not just a matter of belonging to a nation or to a nationality; no creative person can conjure up an unquestioning sense of belonging, except at great cost. (And it is the art that suffers first and most.) If you consider that this was the 1950s, a time that most people refer to as the honeymoon period of the Indian Republic, you can see how it can only have gone downhill from there.

There is something strange about reading this book now. I began by thinking of it as a period piece, for that country seems sometimes to be very far away. However, when Dom is on his way to Nathu La in Sikkim, his conversations with his driver seem to be the stuff of today's world. The Sikh gentleman who is the first voice we hear—other than Dom's own—is still to be found in airport bars and will still be saying much the same things. And the Tibetan Dom is interviewing says, in the voice of the interpreter, that 'he has lost his home. His home is in the country where the Dalai Lama stays, but he is not at home here. If he goes back to Tibet now, the Chinia will shoot him. His brother went back and him the Chinia took and shot.'

Through the veil of Dom's impeccable British accent, through the veil of his translator's inadequate English, we can still hear and relate to the plangent voices of these men, with their freight of love and despair.

Somewhere up in the mountains, somewhere in an airport, they are still saying the same things. That's what makes a book timeless.

JERRY PINTO
Mumbai 2020

A Preface

I was born in Bombay. It is the chief city of western India, and it squats on a forked island encircled by the Arabian Sea. It is a very blue sea, except where the sewers of the city disgorge into it; and above it the smoke of the factories hangs, so that passengers on P & O liners become aware of arriving at Bombay long before they actually arrive there.

My family came from a part of India that had been colonized by the Portuguese, which explains the family name, and also the family religion, which was Roman Catholicism. One of my father's sisters, indeed, became a nun and ended up by being beatified. My parents, however, were not religious. My father was a journalist; my mother was a doctor; both professions tend, I should think, to discourage one from being spiritual. Though my father worked for a British newspaper, he was a nationalist, and many of the people who came to the house when I was a child were nationalists just out of jail, or hiding from the police, or Communists who were officially underground. They taught me to play chess and lent me books. Because by the time I was ten I had read all the Russian novelists, my pet name was Domski.

I was an only child. I was never conscious of being lonely: I found myself very interesting, a vice that has persisted and because even as a child my father was wise enough to allow me complete freedom, I spent hours sitting in a corner of the sitting room listening to the talk of the revolutionaries, the Communists and anarchists, the young writers and the painters. They were thin and poorly dressed, often unshaven, and their dry insistent voices ate up the nights, on the verandah with the stars overhead in the silky black sky, and the splayed paintbrushes of the palm trees daubing the horizon with deeper shadows. All this while I had a secret. I could write. I wrote stories, essays, and poems, but mostly poems. When I was about ten I began to show them to my father's friends. They were all very kind. The novelist Mulk Raj Anand helped me to correct my stories; the painter Manishi Dey did a series of charming little watercolours to accompany my poems. I felt convinced that I was meant to be a writer.

Then when I was ten the first of my journeys began. After that I was to go away from Bombay and come back again and again. My father had been offered an editorship in Ceylon. We spent two years in Colombo, during which I wrote poems, bred dogs, budgerigars, and Siamese Fighters, dabbled in painting, and was lonely and miserable, then we returned to Bombay; my father became the Editor of the *Times of India,* but almost at once we were off again. My mother was ill and so my father was forced to take me with him on his travels. All this while, when he was being father and mother in one, he gave me the same perfect freedom. His only strong moral principle was the only possible moral principle one can have today—that people must be free to choose for themselves; and he held this principle too strongly to modify it in the case of a child. So whenever he went somewhere he would ask me if I wanted to come; and if, as I always did, I said yes, whatever the hazards or the expense or the dangers at the other end, he would take me. In this way, before I was fifteen, I had been with him through Australia and New Zealand, to Indonesia during the first days of Sukarno's administration, to Malaya during the heyday of terrorism, to Indochina when the Viet Minh threw hand grenades in the street outside our hotel in Hanoi, to Bangkok and the densely forested, bandit-haunted Mekong Valley, to Burma and Pakistan, and the borders of Red

China. All this while I watched, and wrote poetry. My dogs and budgerigars died, I gave away my tropical fish, I dispensed with everything but suitcases and the typewriter my father had given me. This typewriter became for me the symbol of my vocation. When I put my fingers on the keys I felt a vibration of pure power. Nobody else seemed to feel this in the finished product until one day in 1954, the poet Stephen Spender visited India. It was the first time I had ever met a real poet. Through the large opaque, sea-coloured eyes of Spender I seemed to see how it might be possible to write poetry. I showed him my poems. He liked them, and said he would publish some in *Encounter*, which he did. Also he asked what I wanted in do. Did I want to stay in India?

No, I said. I had never really thought of it before, but thinking of it now I said no. My family was an entirely English-speaking one. My father and grandfather had been at Oxford. The background of my life had been English. In the streets of India I felt uneasy, knowing neither the language, nor, because of not having come into contact with many Indians who were not from an English background, the people. I suppose I had always known I would leave India, but when Spender asked me if I wanted to, the answer came clear at last.

I left India in 1955. The combined efforts of Spender and my father had gained me admittance to Jesus College, Oxford, but I had a year to kill before going up. I spent this year in Europe: I wandered about in France and Italy, spending a month in Sardinia: then I went on to Greece, spending four months there, including a month in Crete looking for the minotaur. I finished up in Yugoslavia, snowed up in a Belgrade winter. I was staying with a beautiful widow, who used to take me to strange, faintly sleazy basement nightclubs where the opponents of Tito drank rakia, snarling and wiping the frost from their thick dark moustaches. All this while my eyes kept communicating power to my hand, and wherever I was I wrote, on iron tables of cafés, in trains and ships, or sitting on a rock in the sunlight watching the lizards licking their breakfast from the air. Then I returned to England and went up to Oxford.

About this time I met David Archer. He ran a bookshop in Soho. In 1933 he had published Dylan Thomas's first poems, in 1934 George Barker's, in 1935 David Gascoyne's, and in 1942 W.S. Graham's. Now, in 1956, he published my first book of poems. It was called *A Beginning.*

Meanwhile the Hungarian Revolution had broken out and I abandoned Oxford and shot off to the frontier, where I spent a couple of weeks. I returned by way of Germany to find myself in terrible trouble with the university, but also to find my poems a critical success. Finally, in 1958, they were awarded the Hawthornden Prize for the year's best imaginative work. This convinced my college that it would be a mistake to expel me. So they kept me, and in 1959 I became a Bachelor of Arts of Oxford University. If I pay my college dues regularly for three years I shall in due course become a Master of Arts, which would be nice for everybody.

Nobody had ever expected me to finish my three years at Oxford. I was always in trouble. When I felt like going to London, or even abroad, I always went; I brought up trainloads of drunken poets who turned the college into shambles overnight; I didn't turn up for tutorials. My college, however, had endless patience. This was especially due to my principal. He shielded me from the wrath of the disciplinary' authorities. Occasionally, in the quadrangle, he winked at me. We understood each other.

After Oxford was done, I felt a little strange. Mostly because I had fallen in love properly at last, and that confused me, who had always stood alone. My second book of poems was in the press, but I felt I should do something else. I felt I should go somewhere for a little by myself, to think about what loving somebody involved, and become more confident, if I could. I decided to go to India.

This book is the result. It was written with a particular person in mind, who was not with me. It is not really a travel book, nor is it political. It is a journal of what I did and felt during August–November last year, when I happened to be in India. So it may be too personal; but I hope, and I think, that that may be a good thing, because perhaps it makes the work more true.

I owe a debt of gratitude to my father for everything, to Marilyn Silverstone for reading and criticizing the manuscript, to Mr T.R. Gopalakrishnan of the *Indian Express* for typing it, and to James MacGibbon for infinite patience in waiting for it.

London, January 1960 Dom Moraes

Song

I sowed my wild oats
Before I was twenty.
Drunkards and turncoats
I knew in plenty.
Most friends betrayed me.
Each new affair
Further delayed me.
I did not care.

I put no end to
The life that led me
The friends to lend to,
The bards who bled me.
Every bad penny
Finds its own robber.
My beds were many
And my cheques rubber.

Then with the weather worse
To the cold river
I came reciting verse
With a hangover.
You shook a clammy hand.
How could I tell you

Then that wild oats died and
Brighter grain grew?

Now once more wintertime
We sit together.
In your bright forelock
Time gives me good weather.
All true love I know is
Patience and care.
Such grain as I grow is
Hued like your hair.

Going Away

Angst possessed me the afternoon I left for India, with the remembrance of fourteen swans on the Thames, and your bewildering kiss of goodbye. A small grey cobweb of rain covered the London airport. I sat in the bar till three, drinking double brandies, one of the impersonal community of the about-to-depart, masked in magazines. Outside the aeroplanes squatted among meadows of tarmac, looking derelict till their windows were blocked out with small disclike faces and one by one they lumbered into the air. It seemed a long time before ours did, but only a short time before it settled its wings through ridged greyish clouds, and came down on Düsseldorf.

On this interim soil the impersonality of my companions broke down; identities began to appear, like distressing flowers. At the bar a tall Sikh stood drinking whisky after whisky. He offered me a drink. 'It will not be long,' he said, 'before we arrive where we shall not be able to drink at all.' I was not sure whether he meant death or India, but accepted a brandy. He thought I should drink whisky, and muttered rather threateningly, 'Soon you will be glad of anything you can get.' The other passengers were mostly Indian families, the fathers plaintive in brown suits beside their gross wives, and children bleating amidst the debris of their teas. 'Too many children, bhai,*' said the Sikh. 'That

* Brother.

damn country is full of children. What is the use of them? They will grow up and do nothing. Otherwise they will grow up and become damn crooks like their fathers. As for me,' he added, 'my home is in Delhi, where the women are pretty, but I would not marry for anything.' We had several more drinks, and returned in jovial agreement to the aircraft.

On the way to Zurich I sat thinking sad thoughts about love and separation, but was continually interrupted by the Sikh, who now sat by me, discursing like Schopenhauer of the woe that is in marriage, and ordering round after round of drinks. By the time we arrived at Zurich I was in a state of deep alcoholic melancholy. I ordered the Sikh a large whisky in the airport bar with a Byronic toss of my head, and when we got back into the plane fell heavily and completely asleep.

At three next morning I was shaken awake. The Sikh leant over to me, pursing his lips redly through the coarse greyish hairs of his whiskers. 'Cairo.' I looked down, and saw many lights, and scrubby palm trees. We landed with a small succession of bumps. A few minutes later we were in another airport bar. All the children, awakened, were crying; the heavy-lipped mothers in their attempts at solace filled the room with noise. Sad with a hangover and the usual guilt, I suddenly felt extremely irritable. A mother came up to me, lamenting. 'Oh for Christ's sake!' I said. It was as if I spoke only to myself: she did not understand English. I had another drink with the Sikh, standing in the faint chirping night by a dry fountain. 'India is full of crooks,' he said. 'Why are you going back? Nepotism,' he said, and, liking the word, repeated it. 'There is no nepotism in Manchester,' he said, 'I have lived there for three years. A fine place. The cotton business is very good there, no bribery, everything honest,' and I like him felt suddenly nostalgic for the northern cities asleep now under rain three thousand miles away, save perhaps for policemen in wet oilskins alone in the oilskin-textured streets.

It was so gloomy, really, the unfamiliar colour of the night, and the unfamiliar birds ruffling awake as day broke, and stray dogs running across the airfield, and suddenly a haggard man before us with his hand outstretched as though in blessing. 'Beggars,' said the Sikh with contempt. 'Let us go.' I fumbled in my pocket, but he caught my arm. 'No,' he said. 'Give to one and you will get a hundred.' I remembered the phrase: it was the first advice ever given to me as a child.

We took off through the sunrise. The day resolved itself over desert and sea. We had now been joined by a teetotal Arab with a gun. The Sikh gloomed in his beard: I was sulkily quiet. The armies of fathers, mothers, and offspring, however, grew birdlike and sang for joy. They were coming home from a Europe that had not touched them. It had touched me, it had touched the Sikh: we were both apprehensive of the country to which we were coming across the sea, and 'I do not know,' said the Sikh, 'if I will like India. Let us have a drink.'

So we went on drinking till we reached Bombay. We knew when we arrived. The plane struggled down through clouds. Rain sprayed like buckshot over the windows. Winding themselves in their seat belts the passengers began to assume a new impersonality of the about-to-arrive. By the time we touched down they were all strangers again: and when I descended the ramp, though the Sikh was by my side, I was again alone.

We straggled over the puddled tarmac towards the Customs shed. At the edges of the airfield were ragged bushes, barbed wire, and refuse, and, beyond, purple hills helmeted in cloud. It was very hot. I took my jacket off and hung it neatly over my arm. The balconies were filled with brown faces, white clothes, fluttered handkerchiefs: an incessant watery mumble of talk rose from them. Suddenly I recognized my father on the steps of the Customs building.

'Goodbye,' I said to the Sikh. 'I hope all goes well.'

'Same to you, chum,' he said, and then, lifting his long hands in the Indian greeting: 'Ji namaste—go with God.'

~

The airport is ten miles from the city. It takes a long time to get from one to the other. I had forgotten: because the roads, narrow and tree-spiked, are full of people, all wearing white, drifting between the puddles, doe-eyed, sometimes holding hands. Kiosks selling fruit and food abut upon the road. The people did not hurry when the car pressed them from behind. They turned aside in a kind of languid chaos, and as very slowly we passed, stared through the windows, stroking their fingers gently over the sides of the car, red tongues protruding pleasurably between their lips. My father's driver was a bearded young Mohammedan, of a race that likes speed; he shouted hopelessly, blew the horn; his toe trembled above the accelerator, but it was half an hour before we reached the wide boulevards of the residential areas by the sea, and he could bring it down. Progress quickened, and we reached the great block of flats where I was to be installed: looking on the sea, with lawns, terraces, a swimming pool. When we went up the front door of the flat was already open: beyond stood a line of servants in white, each with two fingers to his forehead, 'Salaam, sahib,' they all sang softly at me, too respectful to smile. 'Salaam,' I said, smiling. 'The bearer will look after you,' said my father.

The bearer showed me to my room. 'I run your bath now, sahib,' he said. Gently he clapped his hands, and another servant appeared and ran it. The milieu was luxury, save that the water was dark brown. I did bathe in it, however, and when I emerged found the bearer outside with a drink, my case unpacked, and fresh linen on the bed. 'Dinner ready, sahib.' 'Thanks,' I said, 'I never eat dinner.' 'Young master must eat,' he breathed serenely. So I ate, while a fan hummed and clicked unceasingly overhead. Having to be Young Master gave me a strange sense of loneliness. 'It must be teatime for you in England now,' I thought, 'perhaps with chocolate biscuits. As for me, darling, I must see somebody.' So, after preventing the bearer from dialling for me, I telephoned Mulk Raj Anand.

I used to know him a long time ago, when I was a child. Since then he had become international, and I had seen him twice in London. He was the first Indian writer in English to live in England: he had been a London literary figure in the 1930s, and a friend of Forster and the Woolfs. His novels about the Indian poor had sold well in England then, and sell very well in the Communist countries now. Also, he had become the Editor of a well-known art magazine, and a member of the Indian Academy of Letters.

I had begun to feel neurotically a stranger, so it was a relief to find Mulk welcoming. In his warm husky voice, pleasantly breathless, 'Come and see me,' he said. 'Very soon. Come today if you like. Come tomorrow. You know my flat? Your father's driver knows it.' A pause. 'It is very nice to have you back.' And that comforted me in my state of Young Masterdom. So while still comforted, I retreated into my bedroom.

They had done it up for me. My old pictures had been rehung: there were magazines and a little pile of new novels by my bed (also a number of religious tracts, left by my mother), a flask, cigarettes, nuts, sweets, roses on the bookcase. I sat down on the bed and took my pills, feeling rather overwhelmed. I wondered how the Sikh was finding it all. Then I fished your photograph out of my case and stood you among the roses. I looked at you a long time and decided we both seemed a bit lost. So I put you under my pillow instead, and switched the light off. And was kept awake all night by the rain and the far-off commotion of the sea.

It was still raining in the morning. I was awakened by the cries of strange birds. When I drew the curtains and looked out into a sultry grey light, a hundred little parakeets, studding the dripping branches of the trees outside, sharply flirted their green wings and dived out of sight. I went back to bed to postpone the world. At eleven I remembered Mulk. The bearer helpfully sent for a taxi.

The driver looked curiously at me as I climbed in. I showed him Mulk's address on a slip of paper. 'Do you know the place?'

'Yes, sure,' he said.

The rain had stopped, but the sky was dreary and the streets filled with the same white-clad drifting crowds, apathetic and walking nowhere. We drove away through them, very fast, circled a Parsee fire-temple and several groves of palm trees, and returned to where we had started. The driver turned and smiled at me, pleased.

'This isn't right,' I said.

'Yes, sure,' he replied.

'Ask somebody.'

He asked somebody. Then, in a spurt of enthusiasm, he asked several others. They all gave us different directions. We set off again at great speed. He stopped several times to ask more people. Eventually, after a very long time, we drew up at a large house on the seafront.

'Is this it?'

'Yes, sure.'

I went up the front steps. The door was open, but I couldn't find the bell. So I coughed several times. Then I stamped my feet. Then I coughed and stamped my feet alternately for a couple of minutes. Nobody came. I turned away in despair and found a servant squatting behind me, watching me with interest. He had obviously been a spectator for some time.

'Does Dr Anand live here?'

He did not understand. I shouted the name several times. At last he put his hand gently on my wrist, nodding reassurance, and led me round to the side door. Then he pointed to the stairs and raised two fingers.

'Thank you,' I said.

Two flights up, I found a door and rang. A woman in a sari answered.

'Is Dr Anand in?'

'You have come to the wrong flat,' she said. 'Dr Anand lives on the other side of the house, on the ground floor.'

'I'm awfully sorry. I was told it was here.'

'You should never listen to people's directions in India,' she said briskly. 'They are always wrong.'

Hers turned out right. I found Mulk lying on a sofa in a room full of books, paintings, and a litter of manuscripts. By his side sat a very beautiful woman in slacks, his wife, the dancer Shirin Vajifdar.

'Hullo,' Mulk said. 'It is a long time since you last came home.'

He lay back on the red-covered sofa, small and composed, and his wife sat quietly near him. In the corner of the room a servant knelt, his hands climbing like brown spiders over a heap of books. Outside the garden was drenched with the last rain, shot through with vivid flashes of birdsong, and the crickets worked their small machinery in the grass. I began to feel curiously weightless, with the slow float of a headache. This precluded me from saying anything. With Mulk, however, it did not matter.

'You must write about the commercial film industry here. It's really fantastic. Hardly any of the stars can act, but they get £7,000 for each picture. They shoot six or seven simultaneously, you see. Besides, they only get about £1,000 officially, the rest is black money, paid under the counter, so they can't be taxed on it. The corruption is fantastic. You must write about it.'

'Yes.'

There was a pause, and for a few minutes we exchanged compliments, with gaps of silence: like a ritual dance, advance and retreat. It struck me suddenly that my whole morning had had this ritual quality: as if social intercourse was based on a system of flattery by misdirection: a conception of courtesy between individuals whereby neither could ever possibly be wrong.

'I would like to meet some young writers in Bombay,' I said. 'Could that be arranged?'

'There are none so distinguished as you,' Mulk said. 'In fact,' he added frankly, 'I don't know if there are any at all.'

'None at all?'

'The poets go into films, you see. Writing the lyrics for musicals. Nobody will publish their books, the magazines don't pay for poetry and the radio is not much better. They mostly marry young, they have families and it's all very difficult. Whereas the film people pay enough for the young poets to move out of their hovels in Kalbadevi into five-room flats on Marine Drive. In fact, they pay enough to make them stop writing poetry.

'I haven't read very much,' he added, 'but I can't believe anything important is being done in the Indian languages, except Bengali. Bengal has a living tradition, you see. But the rest of India is dominated by the bourgeois mind. It's a frame of mind that has come in since Independence. The petty moneylenders are the new rich, they despise the arts, the middle class don't bother, the poor are too tired to care. The artist gets no encouragement, anywhere. If you want to write about Indian literature outside Bengal, it would be better to look at the writer sociologically.

'Even among such writers as there are the jealousy is extraordinary. I know the six best Urdu poets. Not one of them will speak to another. The only time they ever meet is when they come here to dinner.'

'Isn't there anywhere else for writers to meet?'

'No,' said Mulk simply.

His wife had vanished, but there was a rustle of silk at the door and when I turned four incredibly beautiful Indian girls, high-breasted, long-necked Leda's daughters, floated their saris past us and were gone.

'My wife's dancing class,' Mulk explained. A shrill plaintive twanging started inside the house, and the tentative tap-tap of drums. 'It's a practice,' Mulk said. 'One of the few consolations,' he added, 'is that we have an evening of music and dance once a week. Otherwise it would be impossible. As it is I spend four days a week in Khandala, doing my writing. The real aristocracy in Bombay now are the film stars and the British advertising executives, and they are both mostly illiterate. It's frightening.'

He was suddenly very serious, moving his hands slowly in the air, as if threading a needle, and frowning with concentration.

'People attack me for being a Marxist. I'll tell you a story. There is a village near Khandala where the caste families evicted forty untouchable families who were trying to build a road. The case was put to the central government two years ago. Nothing has happened.

'When you're dealing with people like that, there is nothing you can do. One could fight the British, but one can't fight them, because they are petty bourgeois, they are nothing, and one can't fight the wind. I have bought two villages, and the untouchables have moved into them. But I can do nothing to get the petty bureaucracy out. If I lived in England I shouldn't worry, because there the bureaucracy seems to work. Here it doesn't, and I protest, and they call me a Marxist.'

We smiled at each other, and he jumped up, suddenly vivacious.

'Never mind. We'll give a party for you, and get some writers to come to it. We shall have some music and a little dancing. Would you like that?'

I said yes, very much, thank you, and could he tell me where to find a taxi, because I must go. Yes, he said, and gave me the directions carefully.

I went out and walked down the seafront. It was coming on to rain again and the cripples scattered along the pavement were huddling down, scaly tortoises, pulling ragged sheets over their heads like shrouds. I turned first left as directed, then first right, and found myself in a blind alley.

I stood and looked into it, in a somewhat ambiguous frame of mind. Mulk had obviously given me the wrong directions.

The Worst Place in the World

The city of Bombay is built on an island. Thus the sea exerts a considerable influence on the life of Bombay, more than I had suspected as a child, when, from the windows of my father's flat, I watched the triangular hills of the fishing boats like a row of teeth on the sea horizon. The cocktail parties to which I now went were always in houses by the sea: along the great boulevard of Marine Drive, or on Cumballa Hill or Malabar Hill. The sea is aristocratic in Bombay, lying under the lighted windows of rich houses, purring to itself and listening to the subdued thunder of cocktail shakers from within. If the sea were not there, one felt, there would be no parties.

The poor live inland, where they can neither see nor hear the sea. Factories spout like whales in the areas where they live, but these whales are marooned on concrete. In the tall narrow tenements around them the poor sleep ten to a room, or sleep on the pavements with their rags drawn up over their faces. They have never heard the cocktail shakers thunder in the corridors, unless they hire themselves out as butlers: and even then, a really poor man has too many lice to be a good butler. This is the folk wisdom of the rich.

These cocktail parties are extremely strange affairs. This is largely because Bombay is a prohibition state. Nobody can drink without a permit, and Indians have to declare themselves confirmed alcoholics before they can get one. You are not legally supposed to drink more than is allowed on your own permit. At some cocktail parties therefore, the host strews empty bottles of drink round the room, one at the feet of each guest. The idea is that if the police raid the party, each guest picks up a bottle and states that he has fetched along his own liquor, off his own permit. The need for such precautions leads to a certain tenseness in the atmosphere, which leads either to a general apprehensive silence or to furious quarrels where husband and wife reproach each other for their infidelities and threaten immediate divorce. Many such parties, of either kind, end in tears.

This, however, applies mainly to cocktail parties given by Indians. There are other sorts. For instance, there are the British cocktail parties. These are populated by executives who tell you yes, they are Oxford men themselves. While in England they live in Dorking or Esher and have elderly mothers. Their wives congregate seedily in a corner talking of their servants. Their skins have gone wrong in the heat and come out in dark splotches. They have all pencilled bright daring scarlet mouths on the ruins, and these mouths talk incessantly in marsh-bird voices. Such parties drag on a long time and end in Dorking gossip. Also there are the American parties, where you drink bourbon on the rocks. The women are cool and smart, and interested in local handicrafts. The men smile indulgently at them, often tell their guests that their wives are the most wonderful women in the world, and discuss office work. This sort of party is sculptured to a beginning, a middle, and an ending. The ending is usually pleasant in the sense that one gets too drunk to notice what is going on.

Apart from cocktail parties, Bombay has no social life, simply because unless you are a diplomat you cannot get enough drink, or you cannot afford enough, to be able to ask people to drop in of an evening. A bottle of whisky, for instance, costs £4 at the legal rate, and £5 in the black market. Moreover, there are no good restaurants, and since in any case you cannot drink with your meals, the atmosphere in such restaurants as there are is one of hopeless gloom. They are, as I imagine, restaurants must be like in an occupied city.

A few days of this made me very grumpy indeed. I spent the mornings in efforts to write, frustrated because it required no effort at all to sweat; the afternoons visiting people; and in the evening death and the cocktail party began again. The people I visited were Mulk, sometimes, who kept urging me to interview film stars; Nissim Ezekiel, a poet who deserves to be better known in England; Arun Kolatkar and Dilip Chitre, two young Maharashtrian novelists who look exactly like Rimbaud and Verlaine. All these, however, also seemed tired and frustrated in their attempts at writing. In each of them one felt a swaddled voice pinioned under the weight of the grits of the city.

Marilyn Silverstone gave me an idea, after these first few days. She is a *Time-Life* photographer, and had had a somewhat tempestuous career during her brief visit to India. Arriving at the time of the Dalai Lama's flight from Tibet, she had gone up to Tezpur, in the NEFA* area, to photograph his arrival. There had been many other journalists there, but Marilyn had gone a little beyond them all, in that, when the Dalai Lama boarded a special train at Siliguri, south of Tezpur, she had hopped aboard with the idea of getting some exclusive photographs. She had promptly been arrested by security police and interrogated for several hours under suspicion of being a Communist spy. Now, safe in Bombay, she became a little heated whenever she thought of this, but tried not to think of it too often. I trusted Marilyn's ideas, for their enterprise, and one evening she said, after I had been delivering myself of a tirade on Bombay: 'Why don't you go to some of these speakeasies, then? See how the other half lives.'

'Now just be careful,' admonished my father.

'It's all right,' Marilyn said sedately. 'They all have police protection.'

---

* The North-East Frontier Agency region of India.

It was discussed for some time, but I had made up my mind, and next day got hold of Marilyn's contact, a stocky, cheerful Indian journalist called Arthur. He arranged to pick me up that evening, and arrived in the original jalopy, carrying a large cloth bag full of empty bottles.

'I like to replenish my stock when I visit these bootleggers, see?'

With him was another journalist, known only by his initials: B.Z. He sat in the back, cheerfully describing his previous experiences in speakeasies, which seemed to be considerable.

'It's all balls about the police,' Arthur said. 'What police will come, man? They are all paid by these fellows, see? True, no, B.Z.?'

'Ah, yes, yes, true,' B.Z. said. 'You will see that, Mr Moraes. Where shall we go first, Arthur bhai?'

'Let us start with somewhere inside the city. He must see everything, no?'

Bombay at night, away from the sea, is curiously exciting. The darkness is bluish and smells of cooking food, excrement, flesh, musk, and oil, all mixed up. Every street is fronted with lighted shops and white-clad men wander hand in hand across the road, twittering and whistling. Cars have to nose slowly through this indolent float of people, their horns snoring in the humid air.

On the edge of the city, where it begins to give in to suburbs, Arthur stopped the car in a crowded thoroughfare. We climbed out into the noise of the street. People bumped gently into one and drifted away again. B.Z. rushed over to one of the shops and returned with three paans. These are a mixture of areca nut, spice, and betel wrapped together in a green leaf.

'Here, chew these. They help to digest the liquor.'

We went up a sidestreet into a decrepit tenement. It was entirely unlighted, and we had to clamber up four flights of stairs. On every landing homeless vagrants were stretched out, asleep. When we reached the top floor there was one light on, in a small room. We entered this. It was partitioned off to make a compartment in the back, from which rose the most extraordinary odour of fermentation and decay.

'That is where they do the brewing,' Arthur said.

The outer room was furnished with two chairs and a large bed, on which lay two small children, asleep. B.Z., chewing his paan, waved me to one of the chairs and shouted for the bootlegger. He emerged, a small corpulent man in underwear, from the brewery. He wore a Catholic scapular round his neck.

'Is he a Christian?'

'Sure,' said B.Z.; 'all these bootleggers are Christians.'

I noticed further proof on the walls. There were three pictures, one of Christ, balancing a raw heart in his hand, one of the Virgin Mary, and one of both together. There was also an embroidered motto. 'Sustain outburden, Lord Jesus,' this said. While I was looking at these and nibbling my paan, which had a sweetish, not entirely unpleasant taste, the bootlegger came out of the brewery again with three thick unwashed glasses and a milk bottle containing a colourless liquid. He slopped a large quantity of this into each glass, and added some soda.

I tasted mine without pleasure. It was rather warm, first of all, as if the bootlegger had been dipping his fingers in it. The flavour was curious, rather undefinable, but not agreeable. A mixture of coconut, rubber, and oil. I drank it very quickly.

'You like?' said the bootlegger, flattered. 'That very good stuff, master. No getting better than that. Two days old.'

'What is it made of?'

'You don't worry, master,' said the bootlegger. 'I no using only very good stuff. Molasses, rotten fruit, coconut, everything I putting. You drinking more?'

I refused, but smoked a cigarette while Arthur and B.Z. finished their drinks. Two government clerks came rather guiltily in just before we left.

'Now,' said Arthur, 'we go to a more high-class place.' The drink seemed to have made him jolly and rather schoolboyish.

'I will fill my bottles there.' We got back into the car and drove on into the suburbs. When we stopped again it was just off the main road, next to a plantation of palm trees.

We went off the road through these palm trees. There was a smell which suggested awful things, and the ground was soft and clinging underfoot, lending confirmation to these thoughts. Somewhere among the palm trees we came to a thatched shack. We went inside. It was again a small room, candle lit, papered with religious mottoes, containing several chairs, a large bed, where again a couple of children slept peacefully, and at one end of the room a crude counter behind which stood a pugnacious-looking woman in a red sari and spectacles. There were several unshaven young men in the room, all wearing white Punjabi pyjamas.

'Urdu poets,' B.Z. whispered. 'When they get drunk you will really hear something.'

A plump young woman in a cotton frock came round with more thick glasses. The liquid she poured out of a hair-oil bottle was brown this time.

'This is what makes this place high-class,' Arthur explained. 'These fellows put colouring in their liquor to make it look like whisky.'

It tasted exactly the same as the liquor at the first place. While we were drinking it, I watched the young poets. They were all sitting, chin in hand, in attitudes of dejection, occasionally drinking with a slight flourish. Suddenly, however, one sprang up, upsetting his chair, and began to shout at the top of his voice. I noticed that the shouting was more or less musical, and seemed to divide itself into lines, and the shouter flung out his hand in a great gesture, worked his eyebrows, and looked out of the corner of his eye to see how his friends liked it.

'Ghalib,'* B.Z. explained. 'He is quoting Ghalib, something about wine.'

---

* The great Urdu poet.

When the first young man had finished another leapt up and also began shouting and waving both his arms. One of the children on the bed woke up and began to cry. The plump girl in the frock rushed over, caught it up, and began industriously breastfeeding it. The poet went on shouting. At the end the others smacked their thighs with loud appreciative cries. A young man in underwear appeared at the outer door, looking surprised.

'That is the husband,' Arthur said. 'He has been watching for the police. It's a cooperative family, see. The girl who serves is his wife, his mother takes the payment, and those are his children on the bed. Have a drink,' he said to the young man, who accepted.

'I must go back soon,' he said.

'No, why, man?' Arthur said. 'The police won't hurt you.'

'Sir, no, but if any come for their payments, I must pay them before they come in here and frighten away the customers.'

'How much do you pay?' I asked.

'Arre, they are like flies. Five-five rupees I pay to the inspectors to keep away. But then every constable in the district comes, and brings his friends also. One-one rupee I must pay to each of them. I must be paying one-one rupee to two hundred constables and their friends every month, and five-five rupees to the inspectors. Altogether three hundred rupees a month I am spending on them.'

'And how much do you take in?' I asked.

'It varies, sir. Six to seven hundred rupees a month. This prohibition is a blessing, sir. Before this I was working as a sepoy for seventy-five rupees a month. Now, even with these sister-raping policemen, I am earning enough to keep my wife and mother and when my children grow up I will be able to send them to school.'

'Well,' I said, 'that's pretty good.'

When he had finished his drink, wiped his hands on his undershirt, and departed into the darkness, we decided to leave. 'At the next place,' Arthur explained, 'we will see a still.' B.Z., who was beginning to get drunk, was in that mood of bitterness that seems to go with drunkenness in Bombay. 'This bloody city,' he said, lurching. 'No fun in this bloody city.' We passed several loitering policemen, to whom he repeated this loudly in Hindi. None of them took any notice. 'The bootlegger pays protection for his clients as well,' Arthur explained. We drove on, deeper into the suburbs. Finally, after parking on the main road, we walked through a muddy lane, lined with palm trees, to another shack.

'A tin roof,' Arthur pointed out. 'This fellow has got so prosperous that he can afford to put in a tin roof instead of thatch. It used to be the best place in Bombay—all the journalists used to come here—till the proprietor took to drinking his own stuff.'

We stopped at the door of the shack. There was a peculiar noise from inside, like someone beating a carpet, mingled with squeals of pain, and then a little fat man curled up like a foetus came rolling through the doorway pursued by a large woman with a bamboo staff in her hand. She landed a final thwack and looked at us, arms akimbo.

'Gustav is drunk again,' she announced.

Gustav jumped up, dusted himself off, and said grandly to his wife, 'Woman, bring liquor for these sahibs.'

'Bring it yourself,' said the wife, and disappeared.

'Women do not know their place these days,' Gustav explained to us. 'However,' he added, 'I will be indulgent this time. I, Gustav, will bring the liquor. Please go inside, do not run away, Gustav flies!' And flapping his arms with many an unconvincing cackle he stumbled off into the dark.

We went in. There were benches and low tables set out in a long room lit by a single oil lamp. By its flickering light two men in their underwear were playing cards in a corner, a bottle between them. We sat and waited. Presently Gustav returned, reeling from side to side, and carrying a bucket. His wife, wordless with disapproval, came out of the kitchen behind the main room with three glasses. She dipped each into the bucket and brought it out half-full of a dubious fluid. 'One for me too,' Gustav carolled, with a shrill giggle. Still wordlessly, his wife stopped, dipped out a glassful, and emptied it over Gustav's head. Then she produced the bamboo and chased him out of the room.

'He will go back to the still,' Arthur said. 'Come and see.'

We went out, leaving B.Z. behind. Gustav could be seen in the distance scuttling across the fields. We followed, stumbling and slipping continually in the darkness. A strong and totally undesirable smell reached the nostrils. 'That is the wash,' Arthur said. We traced it—this was easy enough—to a lean-to in the field. A fire flickered inside. Gustav was squatting by this fire, over which hung a copper bowl. Over the copper bowl an earthenware vessel was suspended, and a smaller earthenware vessel hung above. Dense clouds of steam poured up, making us all blink and choke.

'The copper bowl holds the wash,' Arthur said. 'Rotten fruits, molasses, and all that. The smaller earthenware bowl holds cold water. The steam from the wash condenses on the top bowl and falls into the vessel below. That is what you've been drinking.'

'Have one with me,' said Gustav, owlishly, crouched over the fire.

But we went away.

'The smell!' I said. 'One can smell it a hundred yards away. The police…'

'It's all included in the protection money,' Arthur said cheerfully.

When we got back B.Z. was sitting in silent misery listening to Gustav's wife. The two card players continued with their game, and never looked up. The woman turned appealingly to us.

'You may think I am harsh with Gustav, sahib, but what else can I do? Our customers do not come because he is always drunk and sometimes he forgets to make a new boiling for them. I have to try and keep him in order. Otherwise, sahib, we would both starve.'

'This bloody city,' B.Z. said, shaking his head. 'There is no fun in this bloody city.'

I refused to take Mulk's advice and meet film stars, but when various colleges asked me to lecture I said I would, because I wanted to meet students. The first of my lectures was at what was described as a small college, that had been running for five years. The principal of this college, a worried man with grey hair, met me when I arrived and took me into his study for tea. We passed through several long corridors flanked by huge dismal classrooms packed with noisy students. Paper darts kept flying through the air. An ineffectual professor was saying something from each platform.

'Too many in this college,' said the principal sadly.

'I thought it was a small college.'

'Oh yes. Small it is. But that is comparatively, you see. We have two thousand five hundred students at present.'

'Goodness me, however do you manage?'

'We have two shifts a day, you see, morning and afternoon. Some also come for night classes. No, I tell you, Mr Moraes, there are too many.'

I felt apprehensive about my lecture, more so when I found that four hundred students had turned up, about a hundred of whom were girls. The girls sat in a block, separate from the men. There seemed to be the most extraordinary variety of ages among my audience: they ranged from twelve years old to about thirty.

'Don't you have any age limit?' I asked the principal.

'No, the only qualification is that they must have passed the matriculation before they can come here. Our youngest pupil is eleven.'

He grew sadder still. I began my lecture with a sense of shouting hoarsely across a vast abyss. The students' faces reflected total incomprehension. When I tried to be funny they looked grave. I ended the lecture quickly, and was startled at the volume of applause that came back.

'They are grateful to you,' said the principal, 'for getting them off their morning classes. So,' he added, 'are their professors. Otherwise usually in the morning the students are in a jolly mood; they throw ink-pellets.'

The older and better colleges seemed to produce more disciplined, but also more fatuous students. These colleges, founded mainly by missionaries or rich Parsees in the nineteenth century, are patronized by the richer people: the small new ones cater for the middle class. The poor do not go to college at all. The rich young of the missionary colleges were more Westernized than those in the college I had first addressed: they wore American bush shirts and often had American accents. Also, whereas the other students had said nothing, these were always asking questions. They were not really good questions. 'Have you read James Joyce?' they would ask, and proceed no further.

At one of these colleges I was talking to some students after my lecture when a young African came rather shyly towards me. I had noticed him during the lecture, as he had been the only person in the audience sitting alone. I smiled at him, and he came up a little more quickly. The Indian students talking to me immediately turned their backs, and I found myself alone with the African, who said a little breathlessly, 'I'm sorry to trouble you, but I have a few questions to ask you about life in England.' So I asked him to tea the next day. He said, 'Can I bring a few friends?' and I said 'Do' (in a privileged way) and then he left. The other students immediately gathered round, assuming attitudes of rebuke.

'You shouldn't demean yourself by talking to that hubshee.'*

I was surprised. 'What do you mean?'

'We *never* speak to him,' said a pretty girl. 'You've let us down by doing it.'

'They are not like us,' said a boy. 'They are not civilized.'

'Don't be absurd,' I said.

They were all very hurt. 'It's true. They are all savages in Africa. Some of them are still cannibals. Whereas we have a long history of civilization.'

'And they *look* so horrid,' said the pretty girl, pouting.

---

* The Hindi equivalent of 'nigger'.

'It is not colour prejudice,' one of the boys said. 'It is simply that we are a civilized nation and we do not want our country filled with black savages. They will corrupt our women.'

'Have you ever heard of Sir Oswald Mosley?' I asked.

'No. An Englishman? That is not the point. We are not objecting to Englishmen, but we do not like hubshees.'

The next day I had tea with the African boy, Charles, and three of his friends. They were all from Uganda, and had been studying in India for periods of between four and six years. Two were doing law, and two, including Charles, medicine.

They were all very interested in England, in university life there, and particularly in the colour problem. I said that it sometimes happened that a hooligan minority stirred up incidents, but that the government had always taken strong measures to prevent these, and that the majority of British people had no real prejudice against colour.

'How is it here?' I said finally.

The four looked ruefully at each other, and finally Charles said, 'Not easy.'

'I guessed that,' I said. 'Why?'

Laughter. 'Why do you think? It's not active, nobody ever attacks us physically, but nobody ever speaks to us either.'

'Don't you have Indian friends?'

They looked at one another again, checking over their experiences in subdued voices. Of the four only one had an Indian friend.

'The other students, don't they ever ask you home?'

'When they do that, they only do it once. And usually the reason for their asking us is that none of their family has ever seen an African.'

'Girls are more sympathetic than boys,' Charles said (there was a chorus of sniggers and 'You're telling us, old chap'). 'No, shut up, old chap. They sometimes agree to come out with us or they ask us home, but then it becomes too difficult for them and they give it up. Because if we go out in the street with them everybody stares, sometimes schoolchildren call out "hubshee," and waiters are rude in restaurants, and their families object, and it gets impossible.'

'I think it may be due to the caste system, or what's left of it,' one of the law students said. 'Caste after all began as a colour division. The proof is that even in the south, where the people are as dark as we are, there is prejudice.'

Charles said, 'It is not just in Bombay, but all over India. All our boys have the same story.'

'But,' said one of his friends, 'Bombay is the worst place in the world.' They all laughed quite good-humouredly.

'I don't think it is anything to do with caste, old chap, though,' Charles said. 'I think it's just simple racial discrimination.'

I saw the boys several times after this. I noticed that whenever we were in the street, people tended to stop and stare. One or two always shouted 'hubshee' and laughed, not behind their hands. The boys never took any notice, but walked with their heads up. I thought they were very brave.

'Your interviews are all fixed up,' said my father, 'with Nehru and the Dalai Lama. You'll have to go to Delhi. I have to as well, so we can go together.'

Later it transpired that Marilyn was to photograph various things in Delhi, so we all arranged to travel together.

The bearer packed my bag and dressed me, early one morning. Then he packed for my father and dressed him. Then he formed the servants up in a line at the front door to salute us as we left. It was just like when I arrived.

The sun had not yet come up, and it was a cool morning, but I was not entirely sorry to leave Bombay.

Hurricane in Delhi

One of the first things I saw in Delhi after we arrived, on the road straggling through dust-covered fields for ten miles from the airport to the city, was a camel caravan creaking toward Agra and the Taj Mahal, the camels floating along like elongated dragonflies with turbaned riders aloft. The weather too was Saharan, and the people along the road disposed like Arab tribesmen to siesta or gentle tobacco-chewing, on rope beds outside their huts. They seemed far less mobile than the people of Bombay: it made a change.

New Delhi is a scattered city. Coming from the airport there was a clump of houses here, a clump of houses there, part of a new building project, part of another, the great sandstone facade of a Mughal fort, before finally, in an avenue lined with heat-crimped trees, we reached our hotel.

My room was full of the soft thunder of air conditioners, spreading a coolness as clinging and unhealthy as the heat: to step out into the corridor was like entering a warm bath with all one's clothes on: they were sodden in seconds. Bearers floated on bare feet through the corridors with bowls of ice, answering innumerable bells. I drank some beer, took my shoes off, and lay down on the bed, wiggling my toes.

So I fell asleep for a while. When I went across to my father's room, it was already full of the beginnings of the train of visitors who appear, as if answering the Pied Piper's flute, wherever he goes. An employee of Krishna Menon's was unloading all the latest dirt from the defence ministry: American, English, and Indian journalists were scattered with glasses of whisky all over the room, comparing notes: the telephone kept ringing. I decided to strike out on my own a bit. I knew that Ved Mehta was in Delhi, so I looked up his parents' number and called him.

Ved was at Oxford with me, and came down when I did. He had been at Harvard before that, and he was now on his way back to take up a fellowship there, stopping off to see his parents en route. He has been completely blind since the age of three. I remembered, vividly, the last time I had seen him before he left England: we met in a pub in Chelsea; he was leaving for India the next day, and I, not expecting at that time to be in India myself, convinced him, and at the same time myself, that we would never meet again. The more we drank the sadder we got, it had been one of those evenings; in the end Ved had staggered away into the rain leaving me to console myself at the bar.

I got him on the line, after some trouble explaining my identity to the servant, and an astonished voice said: 'Is that really you, Dommie?' This is the name that I was always called by the more whimsical of my Oxford friends: it was originally given me by a little boy. 'Yes,' I said.

'What are you doing here?'

'I'll tell you,' I said, 'if you come and have a drink with me.'

So we arranged to meet that evening, and I hung up and sat down and tried to decide which group of visitors I should listen to.

Eventually, I joined the group around my father: this was where the official from the defence ministry was holding forth. He was a tall man in military uniform, braid and everything: he had a reticent habit of speech, enigmatic grunts and phrases being followed by long silences before they joined on unexpectedly with other phrases to make a sentence. Each sentence, therefore, took a long time.

In this onomatopoeic, meditative style, like a don constructing some elaborate theory on phonology, he spoke of the disaffection among the armed forces caused by the policy of the defence minister. Krishna Menon had recently made several army promotions over the heads of senior officers. General Thimayya, the commander-in-chief, disapproved of these, the phonologist said. Worse than that, he said, shaking his head at us, the army disapproved. The officers were splitting into parties for and against the newly promoted men: that is, by implication, for and against the defence minister and commander-in-chief respectively.

'Trouble,' said the phonologist. 'There will be trouble soon. You mark my words.'

'What does Krishna Menon gain,' I asked, 'by making all these unpopular promotions?'

'Hm. These fellows…who have been promoted…are mostly leftists. What he wants…in my view…is to have an army manned by leftist officers…behind him…against the time that Nehru dies.' He added: 'He has chosen the worst possible time. We have these damned Chinese…muscling in on the frontier. If he splits the army now…there will be trouble. We can't apply non-violent resistance now… If the peasants lie down in front of Chinese tanks…as they did in front of British tanks…the difference will be that the Chinese tanks…do not stop.'

'I think I'll have a drink,' I said. 'Shall you too?'

I opened my eyes next morning with pain and care, one at a time. I was in a totally strange bedroom. I looked at my watch. It had stopped. But it was broad daylight, and I had a moment when I thought I had amnesia, until certain unmistakable symptoms in my head put me right.

The door opened and Ved came in, looking terrifyingly spruce.

'Ved,' I said, dazedly. 'Where am I?'

'You're in the spare bedroom of my house, dear boy. Don't you remember? No, I don't suppose you do.'

'I haven't done anything awful, have I?'

'It depends on,' Ved replied judicially, 'what you call awful.'

He added, 'You were pretty sloshed when I arrived, Dommie, and you kept talking about the defence ministry. After that you gave a lecture on Anglo-Saxon poetry. I never knew you knew so much about it. Everybody there was fascinated, and there were hundreds of people there. Then I thought a little dinner would be good for you, so we went out. Then came the dog.'

'What dog?'

'We found a stray dog on the street. You wanted to take it into the restaurant for dinner, but they wouldn't let you. But you still seemed to think it was there. In fact you put all your dinner under the table for it. The man at the next table went rushing to the telephone to call up his friends. He wanted to tell them that they ought not to miss it, it was the only time this was likely to happen in Delhi. I told him that if you stuck around here for a few days, Dommie, the novelty would be sure to wear off.'

I buried my head in my hands.

'Never mind. Have a cold shower and some breakfast. Then we have some business. There were a lot of writers who came to meet you, but you didn't give them much opportunity. Unless they've changed their minds, I think we should call on them this morning.'

I had a cold shower and, feeling a little better, came out into the dining room. It was a house of broad, sunny verandahs, and the dining room was just off the largest of these. Outside the day was preparing itself to be hot, in a blue tent over the trees. Inside were Ved's father and mother and his sister-in-law.

I had prepared a little apology, but it was swept away. Ved's mother said, 'Poor boy, are you feeling better? Sit down.' I sat down, feeling I didn't deserve it. The sister-in-law, charming and cool in a pale yellow sari, said, 'Have an egg.'

'Thank you, no,' I said, 'I never eat in the mornings.'

'Yes, I noticed last night,' Ved's father said, 'that you seemed to be on a liquid diet.'

But he was chuckling, and I felt a little better. I had met him in London the previous year, and we talked for a while about that. I drank some coffee, and then Ved, in his most organizing mood, said, 'Come on, dear boy. We'd better start.'

I got up obediently. In the taxi I said, 'Your parents are charming. I do hope I haven't shocked them.'

'Oh no,' Ved said. 'There was only one thing they thought a little strange. When we arrived here last night I introduced you to my mother, and you clasped her hand and said, "I'm delighted to meet you. I've heard so much about you, sir."'

The first of the neglected writers we went to see was Khushwant Singh. He is a novelist, whose books have been well reviewed in England: he lived in Paris for some time, working for UNESCO, and I met him there with his charming wife, five years ago. I remember lunching with them in a restaurant with a huge sign outside saying: 'We speak a kind of English.' He is a rich-natured Sikh, with a curious fierceness and quickness of manner, shading down to a tender understanding.

When the bearer let us in, Khushwant was sitting cross-legged in a chair in the drawing room, writing. He had obviously only just got up, for his beard was still in bandages and he had not put his turban on.

'Who is it?' He peered over his spectacles.' Oh Ved and Dom. Has the Anglo-Saxon expert come to apologize?'

'Humbly,' I said; but Khushwant was laughing.

'Sit down. Have some coffee. It's Cona coffee, and quite good. And excuse me while I put my turban on.'

He returned turbaned and unbandaged. His beard was a little greyer than it had been in Paris, but otherwise he seemed much the same.

'I thought the line you quoted from *Beowulf* which you said described your state of mind in India was a misquotation, perhaps. "The Son of Morn in weary night's decline" you kept saying. *Beowulf* must have changed since I read it.'

'Don't,' I pleaded. 'What are you doing these days?'

'Well, I'm writing a history of the Sikhs. The Ford Foundation commissioned me to do it. Interesting work, you know. And I've just finished a novel. That'll sell in the States, I think: plenty of sex, triangles you know, and all that.'

The coffee was brought and Khushwant poured it. It was very good. 'But there's a new epic waiting to be written about India today, a satire. I don't know if you've been here long. Why, there's a whole novel to be written about the career of X. He's a high official of one of our most important states. He started as a hardware merchant and worked his way down into politics. He has a nose complaint, you know. When he addresses public meetings he quite often stops and gives himself a nasal douche at the edge of the platform. Also he has two sons who go around beating up all his critics and laying false charges against them. There was an ICS man he didn't like, a district judge, whom he had arrested in the fellow's own court. It would make a wonderful novel, really.'

'Are you going to write it?'

'Maybe, some day. Any high official's life would do, not just this one: they are all corrupt, they are all nepotists, and they all have peculiar habits. There's another one who is supposed to put down vice. He goes on an inspection tour of the brothels every week, and generally spends the night in one or the other. But at the moment I want to write about the villages of the Punjab. They are where I was born and bred. They're marvellous, you should go there, Dom, to the villages, anywhere really, though the ones I know best are in the Punjab: they are the last outposts of civilization in this country. The peasants are great rough Sikh labourers and artisans, and they talk in a picturesque, highly coloured kind of speech, and swear very variously and frighteningly well. They are rather like peasants were supposed to be in the Ireland of Synge and Lady Gregory.'

'Those peasants didn't swear.'

'True. But, you know, I would prefer to be in India now, as a novelist, than anywhere else. I would prefer as a man to be somewhere else, but as a novelist, no.'

'I saw Mulk Raj Anand in Bombay,' I said. 'He was saying how difficult it is for a writer to live here, because he has no other writers to talk to, and the atmosphere is depressing, and all that.'

'I don't see why it should be. I don't see many writers, but then I don't very much want to. I think life in cities in India is hell, certainly, because the whole country is administered by a bunch of corrupt puritans who operate in the cities. But I get away into the villages quite often, and there are always a few people one knows and likes anywhere one goes. And there's so much material. From that point of view this sort of country is far preferable to England, say. The London novelists write city novels, sex and sorrow and a lot of psychology for padding: novels about a certain way of life. In a country like India one has the material of life itself.'

We talked about Chelsea, where Khushwant used to live in London, and about Paris. He talked without a trace of nostalgia, but with that almost crude realism that is one of the most striking things about his novels. It seemed to me, as we went away, that his was the only possible attitude that a writer in England could take up in India, and live. Though, I thought, to take up this attitude one would need to have the things Khushwant had: a private income, comfortable circumstances, deep roots in the villages, and an interest in many other things beside literature. Without these, one would be forced to share in the general death.

Narayana Menon lives in a cool second-floor flat with a huge drawing room, furnished with broad couches and comfortable chairs, the walls palisaded with paintings by modem Indian painters. He waved his long hand towards one and said in his light and gentle voice: 'Do you like that? Husain's latest. He painted it only the other day. I think it's good, don't you? Come and sit down. No, no, don't apologize. There's nothing to apologize for. Will you have some gin or some beer?'

He is a slight, grey-haired man, with horn-rimmed spectacles on a thin mobile face. He has written a book of criticism on Yeats; during the war he was with the BBC in London, and he now runs the Indian radio network from Delhi.

'You've just been to see Khushwant? How was he? Was he very angry about the news?'

'What news?'

'Hasn't anybody seen the papers? The Chinese came into Indian territory today.' He picked a newspaper up and read from it. 'They crossed the border in the Subansiri division in NEFA, opened fire on our checkpost at Longju and overran it. Three of our boys have been killed.'

'What do you think Nehru will do?'

'Nothing. Protest. Take it as an aberration. In a couple of weeks they'll probably cross into Sikkim or Bhutan, one of those places. More aberrations. Then perhaps they'll cross into some other frontier territory. Ladakh. Then perhaps Nehru will think it has got beyond aberrations and send to the UN for a psychologist.'

'It's a bad time for this to happen, isn't it, with all this dissatisfaction in the army?'

'Well, yes. Though I doubt if the dissatisfaction will get beyond grumbling.'

The servant brought in gin-and-limes and a pretty little girl came in behind him.

'My daughter, Mala,' Narayana said, and his face grew gentler than ever as he watched his daughter say 'How do you do?' and go and sit down with the unique unobtrusive mannerliness that some Indian children have.

'She likes to hear me practise.' Narayana was also a famous veena player. We said, 'Why don't you? We'd love to hear it.'

'Would you really?' Narayana smiled. 'Mala, fetch the veena.'

The little girl's face lit up, and she dashed out and came back carefully carrying the wooden instrument in her arms.

The veena is shaped like half a pumpkin on a stick. The strings are of silver, and strung crosswise across the pumpkin-face. Narayana twiddled a few keys, tautening the strings, then bent over the instrument and began to play it. The long, very flexible fingers of his left hand struck the strings slowly, and a long-drawn-out succession of notes, like the calls of a mechanical bird, filled the room. Each faded out and was imperceptibly replaced by another, or overlapped and sang at different ends of the same golden bough. Mala leant forward in her chair with her eyes fixed adoringly on her father. The servant came and stood voluptuously at the door, his knuckles to his teeth, his eyes half-closed, moving a little with the music. When Narayana finished he looked up at us and laughed. 'Did you like that?'

We nodded, and he said, 'I did some experiments over the BBC during the war: playing European composers on the veena. They were quite successful, though of course there were some composers one couldn't do it with. But I've always wanted to try it the other way round: Indian music on European instruments. That would be more difficult, of course.' He stroked the stained wood of the veena affectionately.

'These things take about six months to make. Hand made, of course. There are only a few craftsmen left in south India who know how to make them. This one is thirty years old. I have another which is nearer a hundred.'

We talked for a little. Then Ved asked if Narayana had read the book by Nirad Chaudhuri, *A Passage to England,* which had been getting excellent reviews in the English press when we left.

'Yes. At least, I found I couldn't finish it. But it's well written. Chaudhuri, you know, has been praising the English way of life for years; but he had never been out of India till this visit of his which produced the book, and then he only stayed five weeks. So it's rather a lopsided book, I think, almost a pathetic book. And certainly most of the reviewers here haven't been very nice to it. One of them said Chaudhuri was like a dog trained to wag its tail when its master said "England." But of course the reviews were pretty lopsided too.'

'Do you know him?' I asked. 'I'd like to meet him. What's he like?'

'He used to work in All India Radio for a bit, and I knew him then. He's an eccentric, you know. He has the most extraordinary fund of information: he knows the date of the founding of Prague, and what porridge John Keats had, and things like that.'

'How does one contact him? Is he hard to see?'

'No, I'm sure he'd be delighted. I should think he feels a little lonely in India. I don't know where he lives myself, but ring up Khushwant and ask him, he would know.'

We said goodbye to him and to Mala and went down to our taxi. Narayana waved to us from the window.

'Ask your father what he thinks of the Chinese attack.'

When I got back to the hotel I found Marilyn in her room chuckling over the matrimonial advertisements in one of the newspapers. This is the modern form of arranged marriages: instead of having an astrologer as a go-between, as they did before, orthodox Indians now use the advertisement columns.

'What's so funny?'

Marilyn read out one of the advertisements between chuckles. 'Wanted one vegetarian virgin, skilled in H.H. affairs, for twenty-year-old cleanshaven bachelor. Caste no bar.'

'What on earth are H.H. affairs?'

'House Hold,' said Marilyn, and giggled furiously.

I went on to my father's room. It was filled with journalists and government officials, as usual: Connery of *Time-Life,* Atkinson of the *Daily Mail,* and in one corner, like Buddha in white ducks, Vincent Sheean. The telephone was ringing, as usual: as usual my father was doing several different things very efficiently, all at once.

While I was getting myself a drink I gathered that Nehru had just made a statement in Parliament over Longju. He had disclosed that for over a year China had been in possession of large tracts of Indian territory in Ladakh; that the Chinese had in fact built a road between Gartok in Western Tibet and Yarkand in Turkestan, that ran through the Aksai Chin of Ladakh and cut off hundreds of square miles of Indian territory; that they had established a military base at Spanggur in Ladakh, and a month before arrested a reconnaissance party sent there by the Indian government. Only three weeks ago, they had attacked the Indian post of Khinzemane, in the NEFA area, and pushed Indian troops back. Altogether they now controlled over a thousand square miles of Indian territory, and had recently announced their intention of making Nepal, Sikkim, and Bhutan, the independent border states, into part of the great motherland of China.

Nehru's speech had come as a bombshell. Everybody had known that there had been Chinese incursions into Indian territory before Longju, but nobody had realized their extent. My father was snorting like a warhorse that hears the trumpets.

'Why hasn't he said all this before? He's kept it a secret for a year. Why hasn't he taken any action?'

'Nehru is not a young man,' one of the Indian journalists said. 'And he has never faced this kind of situation before. He must be trusting in the goodwill of the Chinese not to come any farther.'

An American said, 'It's strange that he should trust the Chinese so much that he hasn't even told his own people and his own Parliament about all this for a year.'

They were all in that peculiar state of exaltation that marks good journalists when history is happening round their ears. For journalists operate in history, as poets operate in time. Both have an acute awareness of the past and of the present, and perhaps of the future: but whereas for the poet these are three separate cells, which with the lucky word he may make one, the speed of history sends the journalist skating forward through all three. Today the only one who did not seem to be skating upon history was Vincent Sheean; he sat calmly in a corner, occasionally joining, trumpet-tongued, in one of the many little arguments in the room, but part of none. I went and sat by him.

'Why don't you go up to the border states?' he said. 'You're young and footloose and you can afford to do it. Go and see what they're like, because in a year's time the Chinese may have got them.'

I said I would think about it.

India's troubles did not seem to come singly. When I awoke next morning, the bearer handed me the newspaper with an expectant look. Banner headlines announced the resignation of the three Indian Chiefs of Staff: Thimayya of the army, Katari of the navy, and Mukerjee of the air force.

I galloped round to my father's room to find him in pyjamas, a cup of coffee in one hand, and the telephone receiver in the other. When he had finished, 'Is this true?' I asked him.

'I don't know. If it is, it will probably be the first time in history that all three Chiefs of Staff have resigned simultaneously in any country. There'll be hell to pay for Krishna Menon. I hear he's furious this morning. He keeps chasing people out of his office.'

It was a pretty picture, but I did not dwell on it. 'What about Thimayya?'

'He isn't saying anything: except that the report came as a great shock. There must be some truth in it: but I think something's gone wrong somewhere.'

Then Marilyn arrived, then Sheean arrived, then Ved arrived, and then came the journalist armies, and the suite began to take on the aspect of an audience hall.

We all waited for the news from Parliament. The prime minister was absent. Krishna Menon was there, fobbing off furious volleys of questions from the opposition. Rumours were running all round the capital, and all the while Nehru kept silence and Thimayya kept to his tent. At four o'clock the news came through that Air Commodore Mukerjee, in London, had denied the rumours of the resignation. Admiral Katari was unavailable to anybody. Things were building up, however, for Krishna Menon.

Next morning the newspapers unanimously denounced him. Some demanded his resignation. The prime minister was to speak at midday. Marilyn shot off to Parliament with her cameras. My father went off with a host of excited French journalists. But Ved and I stayed in the hotel, drinking beer and eating pretzels. 'This is what I shall be doing in America,' Ved said. 'All this resignation business seems silly though. I don't know why people fuss so much about politics.'

Marilyn returned at one, dusty and exhausted, the cloth bags full of cameras swinging from her shoulders.

'Well, everybody said Nehru liked Krishna Menon, and this is the proof.'

'What happened?'

'He said that he had spoken to General Thimayya, and there was no question of his resigning. He said he had gone into Thimayya's grievances and found them extremely trivial.'

'Poor Thimayya,' Ved said. 'Did you get any shots?'

'Yes, I got two very good ones. One of Krishna Menon going into Parliament, looking like a thundercloud. And another of his coming out: and then he looked like a cat that had just eaten a sparrow.'

All the gossip in New Delhi is political. This is because it is not a residential capital, like London; it is a political capital, like Canberra. Most of the richer people are employed in one branch of government service or another, and around them the journalists buzz and whisper. Thus in times of comparative quietness the drawing rooms are filled with rumours of the impending fall of this minister or that minister; of who has Nehru's ear at the moment; of why the American ambassador went to dinner with the minister of food. In times like the one we were passing through, every rumour develops three heads and squirms through the teacups and the cocktail glasses, dipping a different head in each.

So there were many stories about what came to be known as the Thimayya affair, all entirely different. The one that seemed most reliable came from the phonologist in the defence ministry.

According to this story, the split between Krishna Menon and his Chiefs of Staff had grown wider and wider. In particular that between the defence minister and the army chief had assumed the proportions of an abyss. This was mainly over the promotions made by Krishna Menon, but another cause was alleged to be that Thimayya had asked that the Indian troops on the NEFA border should be supplied with automatic weapons, as they were inadequately armed in case of Chinese attacks. This request Krishna Menon is said to have refused: then came Longju, when inadequately equipped and outnumbered Indians were put to flight by the Chinese. Meanwhile Nehru is supposed to have summoned Thimayya on some other matter, and during the course of the discussion asked him whether the disturbing reports of dissension in the army were true, and what had caused such dissension. Thimayya answered frankly, and Nehru told him to go and see Krishna Menon.

When Thimayya arrived at the defence ministry, however, according to the story, he found Krishna Menon in a passionate rage. Thimayya was accused of deliberate treachery and of going over his minister's head. Krishna Menon is further alleged to have said that Thimayya should be behind bars.

At this Thimayya offered his resignation, and Krishna Menon told him he could do what he pleased. Thimayya is then said to have written a letter of resignation to Nehru. This reached the prime minister the next day. He summoned Thimayya, and asked him, in the interests of the country, not to resign. Thimayya accordingly withdrew his resignation and went home.

But that evening someone said something to somebody, and the next day the story broke. Thimayya's alleged reaction of shock is, in this context, understandable: by the time the report of his resignation appeared, he had already withdrawn it. But the whole thing had been dragged out into public, and in a public forum, if not in public opinion, Thimayya had suffered something of a setback. Yet Krishna Menon's victory, if one can call it that, was a Pyrrhic one. In the meantime, however, the gossip still went on, mingled now with a growing movement in the press urging that India should take up the Dalai Lama's case at the UN, and with news flashes stating that Chinese troops were moving along the Chumbi Valley on the Sikkim–Tibet border, that there was Chinese infiltration in Ladakh and Bhutan, and that Chinese troops edging along the NEFA border had replied when questioned that they were an entomological expedition in pursuit of rare butterflies.

All this was going on simultaneously when I went to see Nehru.

The Still Centre

In any shop or business office you enter in India, there are always two guardian angels brooding from gilded frames over the cashier. One is Gandhi, always, in these photographs, venerable, and the other Nehru, frozen into perpetual youth. Beautiful, young, he fills the gilt frame, one hand outflung to an invisible crowd beyond. One can feel this crowd vibrating outside the photograph, not quite getting what Nehru is saying but believing it anyway, because it is Nehru. When the outflung hand is lowered there will be yet another repetition of the thundered cry that has followed Nehru from podium to podium in India these thirty years: '*Jawaharlal ki jai.*'*

Today, after thirty years, the glass of the photograph has cracked. Long after I met Nehru in Delhi, I watched him address a crowd on the sea-beach at Bombay. Three hundred thousand people came through the rain to see him, not in real confidence but in vague hope that the ancient panacea would stream in under their umbrellas from the platform. Yet the moment Nehru began to speak, there was a disappointed murmur; the crowd seemed to realize that they had heard this before. The gathering began to fray apart and dissolve back into the rain out of which they had come: they were obviously all too aware that there would be no panaceas any more.

---

* Long live Jawaharlal.

There are several causes to account for this loss of grip. The most important is the failure of Nehru's foreign policy. Most Indians agree that India's line should be one of non-alignment: but not non-alignment as Nehru sees it. When the West does something wrong, he attacks: when it is the Communists, he always hesitates. Thus he condemned the Suez war and the Algerian butchery in the strongest terms; but he shilly-shallied about Hungary and he glossed over Tibet. He gave the Dalai Lama refuge, but he stipulated that the Dalai Lama should not use India as a political platform. The young and beautiful Nehru of the shop photographs, had he been exiled from his own country at the age of twenty-four, would have been very annoyed indeed if the country that gave him asylum had not also afforded him a political platform.

His economic policy has also brought protest, even from the small farmers who were the wall at his back in the old days. Nehru envisages a system of kolkhozes like those in China and Russia. His economic policy is tending more and more towards regimentation.

Ved and I had been lecturing to several colleges in Delhi. The students here were more sophisticated than those I had met in Bombay, and they talked a little more. I noticed that most of them were either Communists or left-wing Socialists, and I wondered why. One of them explained to me:

'We have all hero-worshipped Jawaharlal for years. We could even forgive him the mistakes he has made in the past, if he only showed signs of changing. But he has surrounded himself with misguided people, and they have fixed him in his course. He is too old to change. Therefore we have swung left, because there is nobody on the right of Nehru, and Nehru himself we do not want.'

Much later, students in Calcutta attacked the prime minister in much the same terms. The students have always been for Nehru, and their shift to the left is a sign that should disquiet the Congress Party. The illiterate electorate, which is in fact the majority, will probably still vote for it, because it is Nehru's party, and voting for Nehru has become a habit, and besides there is no other comparable figure. But the students criticize him; the newspapers attack him almost daily, his own ministers complain (behind his back) that he is dictatorial and will not take the advice of anybody except Krishna Menon, perhaps the most unpopular politician in India: the intelligentsia, such as it is, has forsaken Nehru, and it is sad, because he is still, and in spite of everything, the only man who could hold India to a stable democracy.

It was another hot day. Parliament was going into session at twelve, to try and tidy up the debris of the week's hurricane. My appointment with Nehru was for eleven-thirty. I arrived at quarter past eleven at his secretary's office in Parliament House.

This was a large room, flanked with filing-cabinets. Nehru's secretary sat in one corner behind a desk on which a telephone made constant small jangles. He nodded to me. 'Please take your seat.' One of the three armchairs in the room was already occupied by a stocky and worried-looking man in the national costume of jodhpurs and long white jacket. 'One of our ambassadors,' the secretary told me. From his looks he must have been a very peccant one indeed.

I took my seat, trying not to look at the ambassador, who was breakfasting off his fingernails, and lit a cigarette. Outside the room was a garden filled with tulips; between the garden and the room ran a broad corridor, culminating in tall mahogany doors with brass handles; a red-turbaned sepoy was on guard outside Nehru's office. The prime minister had not yet arrived.

Suddenly there was a stir at the door. Nehru stood in the corridor, a slight, stooped figure in immaculate white jodhpurs and high-necked jacket, a white Gandhi cap on his head. He wore in his buttonhole the red rose that has become a kind of badge of office, and in his hand carried a short sandalwood stick. Everybody in the room jumped up like clockwork. The ambassador, who seemed to have swallowed a fingernail, choked.

Nehru saw me, and lifted his stick to me with a smile. Then he looked coldly at the ambassador. It was eleven-twenty-three. 'I can spare you seven minutes precisely.' He walked through the tall doors that the sepoy had flung open, followed by a train of peons with files. The ambassador, a little sheepishly, brought up the rear.

The secretary winked at me. I smiled, nervously, back.

At eleven-thirty sharp the mahogany doors swung open and ejected the ambassador. A bell rang imperiously at the secretary's desk. He turned to me and nodded. The PM will see you. Go in, please.'

'This is terrifying,' I thought, but went into the corridor and towards the door. The sepoy clicked his heels, snapped into a salute, and opened it. I went straight through and became inextricably entangled in a curtain which I had not noticed on the other side. The door shut firmly behind me.

I struggled free of the curtain and confronted Nehru. He had risen from his desk, and was staring at me with a mixture of wonder and concern. He had taken his cap off. I looked at the high-domed, bald head, the beautiful face with its long, ambitious upper lip and hooded eyes, and said rather foolishly, 'How do you do?'

Nehru said gravely, 'Hullo.' He gave me a rather limp handshake and sat down again. His desk, an enormous teak desk, was set at right angles to the door. I sat down near him, on his left, facing the fatal curtain.

There was a long silence. Nehru had turned sideways in his chair, his fingers playing with a silver paper knife. He looked much older without his cap: one saw the deep lines in his face, and his eyes were more hooded even than one had thought, and entirely abstracted. I didn't know where to begin, so didn't say anything.

Finally, glancing at me for a moment, and then looking back past me to the tulips in the garden, he said, 'I've read your book.'

His voice was so soft as to be almost inaudible, but he spoke very slowly, with long pauses as if he were thinking each word out. There was another long pause, and I was just going to say something when he began again. I noticed later that this long pause occurred between nearly all his sentences.

'What are your plans now? Have you finished with Oxford?'

I said yes, and that I had another book of poems ready for the press, and was thinking of writing a book about what I did in India. He nodded.

'There have been a lot of books written about India.' He turned to me fully for the first time, with a small, fleeting smile. 'I've written some myself.'

'Yes, sir,' I said, and then, 'do you write much nowadays?'

'Not for the last fifteen years. There was no time. Going abroad…state affairs…that sort of thing. I did publish a bunch of old letters a little while ago… If I have time I can always go and dig some more up… I've got files full of the wretched things.'

I recalled an essay of his that I had once read about the Spanish Civil War. It was written in a peculiar succession of images that recalled a masculine Virginia Woolf. I asked him if he remembered it.

'I don't know.… I wrote so much in those days.…'

'If you hadn't been what you are, sir, do you think you would have been a writer?'

He seemed to wake up fully for the first time. He smiled with a swift and extraordinary interest that changed his whole face so that suddenly he looked young.

'That's an intriguing question.… I don't know what I would have been. What I wrote I wrote because it seemed politically necessary, or necessary to me to clear up a political confusion in my mind. I wasn't a poet, a creative writer, I was a political writer. I don't know…perhaps I would have been a scientist. Or a writer…? Yes, perhaps I would have been a writer.'

He turned back and again looked out of the window. In repose his face seemed old, petulant, and disinterested. But when he glanced at me again it lit up with that remarkable smile.

'What do you do in the afternoons? Don't you find it hot?'

I was rather taken aback, but before I could answer he said, 'Do you take your own advice, and choose the wise alternative to death, a nap in the afternoon?'

I recognized two lines from an old poem of mine. I was flattered but again at a loss for anything to say. Nehru said suddenly, bending away from me once more and looking out of the window: 'If you are going to write about India, you must decide which India you are going to write about.'

He looked at me. 'Well?'

'I don't know. I thought I might go up to the Tibetan border states.' For a moment he looked seriously displeased. The eyes hooded themselves like a hawk's eyes; the silver paper knife was tapped on the desk several times in quick succession.

'The Tibetan border states? Why?'

'I would like to have a look at them, sir.'

'Have a look at what?' Then again he back-pedalled, turned and looked out of the window at the stiff marching lines of tulips. He obviously did not want an answer, so I remained silent.

Presently he turned back to me. 'For natural beauty, mountains, that sort of thing, I would say…go to Kashmir and Kerala. I have…a local interest in Kashmir…being a Kashmiri. But it's very beautiful…the mountains…the snow…' I noticed he seldom made any gestures at all, except to fidget with the paper knife.

A peon came in with a file. He put it down on the desk, salaamed deeply, and withdrew. Nehru turned and began to read the file, initialling and signing each page. As he did so, however, the soft, slow voice continued to talk.

'Kerala…is the opposite of Kashmir. Scenically, and all that. But it is a most beautiful part…. There is no point in going anywhere in India and staying in a hotel, except in the cities. You must go to the villages. India is a poor man's country…a villager's country.'

He finished initialling the file and dabbed impatiently at the bell. The peon came in and took the file away. While this was happening Nehru again gazed out of the window, tapping the paper knife on the arm of his chair. He turned to me, but seemed for a moment to have lost the thread of his argument. Then he continued. 'You must go to the villages and live with the villagers. You must accept them for what they are. They are good people. It is difficult for people like you...people from Oxford and Cambridge, coming back to this country...to make that adjustment...because you are too sophisticated, that sort of thing...you have a preconceived notion of what you expect in the way of conversation and comfort.'

'You seem to have made the adjustment all right, sir,' I said.

He smiled again. 'Have I? I don't know.... Yes. I had to...at first it was part of my work, as a young man, and then I loved doing it. I suppose urban students in India would have the same trouble if they went back to the villages...it's unfair to attack people who have studied in England.'

I thought of an incident that had taken place during one of the lectures Ved and I had given. We had arrived at a college to find ourselves addressing the staff. No students were present at all. After the lecture I asked the principal, rather bewilderedly, where the students were. Couldn't we meet some? 'Oh no,' said the principal in a shocked voice. 'They are too badly educated to meet you.'

I told Nehru this story, thinking it terrifying but rather funny, and was rather distressed when he didn't laugh. Instead he turned angrily to his desk. 'Ridiculous,' he said, 'quite ridiculous.' He seized a pencil. 'What was the name of this college?'

I told him, and he scribbled quickly on a piece of paper.

'Quite ridiculous,' he said again, then smiled and added, 'haven't you seen any better colleges than that?'

I said I didn't like what I had seen of Indian colleges: too many students, too few teachers, too little contact between the two, and so on. 'I agree. But the country must have an educated majority.'

'Yes, sir, but at this rate the country's going to have a half-educated majority, which I should think is pretty dangerous.'

'We are still a young country.... All that will come in time.'

I felt a little disappointed in this reply, but looked at the clock, which said twelve.

'I'm sorry if I've kept you, sir.'

He followed my glance. Then he said, 'Parliament can wait for a few minutes.' After this he said nothing for a while, but sat gazing past me at the tulips.

Here, at the still centre of the hurricane that had just swept Delhi, everything seemed orderly but vague. The shadowy room was undecorated except for a few photographs, unfurnished but for the great teak desk and a sofa in the corner. Nehru sat with chin in hand for a few minutes. Then he put the paper knife down on the desk, picked up his cap and stick, fidgeted with a file and said, 'I haven't been able to read much modern poetry in the last fifteen years. Sometimes I wish... I had more time.' He rang the bell and a peon came in and picked up some files. The Cambridge voice shifted suddenly into a beautiful classical Hindi, giving orders. Then he turned to me. 'Sorry, but I must go.' He put his cap on. His face looked younger when he had it on. He put the stick under his arm and waved me through the door ahead of him.

'I'm sorry if I've taken up too much of your time, sir.'

'No, no, my dear chap. Glad to see you.' He patted me on the shoulder, gave me another limp handshake, and then walked off, slight, stooped, and beautiful, followed by a train of peons with files. The still centre moved off towards Parliament, and the regathering hurricane.

Out of a Journal

This morning Delhi is swept by the loose, wild rain that always follows days of heat and thunder. Frogs appear in ditches that have been dry for days; the awnings of the hotel bubble and drip; the trees turn green. 'God in his mercy has sent this'—Vincent Sheean, looking mock-solemnly at the sky—'It will cool Panditji's brow.' The lassitude of the last few days lifts from me. I occupy myself making and shaking Bloody Maries and Old Fashioneds in thermos flasks, Marilyn acting as taster, solemnly waggling her eyebrows in approbation. Wet journalists came into my father's room, but the rain seems to have broken a thread in the air. The talk is no longer of Nehru and Krishna Menon but of the weather.

I want to see Nirad Chaudhuri. Chaudhuri has no telephone. So I ring and ask Khushwant for the address. He seems a bit vague; somewhere near the Kashmiri Gate, he says, but if we go there and ask for Nirad Chaudhuri anyone will direct us: he is a known and beloved figure in the vicinity. Ring Ved, who picks me up in a taxi after lunch.

A long drive to the Kashmiri Gate: meanwhile the sun gropes through the clouds and the afternoon fills slowly with heat. When we reach the Kashmiri Gate, we stop the taxi and ask a passerby where Nirad Chaudhuri lives. He does not know. Conclude that he is not a local inhabitant and push on. An area of exceedingly tortuous streets all mixed up like grandmother's knitting. Heat-haze after the rain, making the road look as if it were covered with oil, and clouds of flies everywhere. Send the taxi driver to inquire at various shops, but draw a blank. Get out ourselves. Swarms of children immediately surround us. 'King of the world, give me money. My mother is dead, my father is dead.' We hold out some coins, they are snatched from our hands and all the children begin to fight over them, tearing one another with their nails. Their small bodies are like relief-maps, so far do the bones stick out.

Ask a photographer (Sikh) where Nirad Chaudhuri lives. He pushes his turban forward and scratches his head like a Mummerset man. First time I have ever seen a Sikh do this, and I watch in fascination. Finally takes his hand away from his head, fingernails coated in oil and scurf, and says do we mean a tall youth called Chaudhuri who goes to school? No, we say, but perhaps his father. His father, the Sikh says, is a lentil-seller by the Gate. No, we say again. The Sikh goes back to scratching his head. Then he asks is it an old man called Nirala? No, we say, a middle-aged man called Nirad Chaudhuri, a writer. Ved adds that he is a Bengali. The Sikh snaps his fingers triumphantly. 'Oh, that fellow! The Bengali Babu!' He gives us directions. As we drive off he runs after us shouting that if we ever want our photographs taken his is infinitely the best shop in Delhi.

Reach Chaudhuri's house, tall and wooden in a crooked street off the Kashmiri Gate. Climb three flights of groaning stairs. It is now very hot and my shirt is damp and heavy with sweat. Ved has a suit on and is worse off, but refuses to remove his jacket because he is wearing braces. By the time we reach the top floor we are both in a vile temper. We emerge into a broad verandah where a naked figure is asleep on a sheet. Ved bends and shakes it impatiently. 'Hai mai, brother, get up and call your master.' Figure springs up, wraps the sheet round itself to form a waist-cloth, and says with dignity, 'I am Mr Chaudhuri.'

Ved and I are dumbstruck. Chaudhuri, however, seems to take it all in his stride. 'Mr Mehta and Mr Moraes? I have seen your pictures in the papers. Please come in.' The main room is spacious but a little bare, the corners filled with heaped up books. Chaudhuri disappears for a moment, reappearing in a shirt and trousers. He is a small frail man with a sharp bespectacled face and a tiny moustache. We ask him about his new book.

'Oh I am *very* pleased about that. *Very* pleased. It has got some fine reviews in England. The English will understand such a book, you see. But here it has got bad reviews, of course. Here they do not understand.'

He gestures frequently, bobbing his head as he makes his points.

'You will not believe it, the Indians do not want to know me. No! It is the foreign diplomats who are my friends. I have been to ten parties in the last fortnight—*all* given by foreign diplomats! Now will you believe that? Is that not extraordinary? I get on better with foreigners, you see. I understand foreigners. Now one of my friends is in the French embassy. His is the last party I have been to. How tastefully his house is decorated! How gracious is the way in which he lives! Every man can be judged by his habits and surroundings at home.'

Ved and I remain silent. Chaudhuri continues: 'I am now writing a book about India. That also will be appreciated in England and attacked here. But I feel that if I write three or four books, perhaps I may achieve some reputation in England. Is that so? If you write three or four books do you achieve a reputation in England?'

I say cautiously that it depends on the books. Chaudhuri is very eager to know more. 'I want to settle in England, you know. I was only there for five weeks, in 1955, but I felt as if my whole life had been a preparation for those five weeks, and after that I feel myself at a loss till I can return.'

He says: 'How beautiful is Hyde Park! And there is so much tradition there in England! The eating places are like palaces—Lyons', the ABC. I feel at a loss for words. It seems to me a totally new view of London. If we had met in London I would have thought this a mad kind of poetry; here, with the Kashmiri Bazaar teeming below, the whole thing seems grotesque. I relapse into silence, while Chaudhuri talks to Ved about literature. He thinks *A Passage to India* Forster's worst novel because, he says, it was improbable: during British days a person like Aziz would never have been able to ask Miss Quested and Mrs Moore to tea or to picnics. He very gleefully adds that he had pointed this out to Forster. Forster, he says, had taken his point.

When we leave he says earnestly: 'I am glad to have met you, but take my advice, and return at once to England. If you stay here you will perish. They will not understand you here.'

Amongst the American journalists who drop in for a drink in the evenings is one with a statuesque and improbable dignity: when very drunk his upper lip trembles a little, as though he wanted to cry. He is to leave this morning and comes in to see my father but remains to breakfast with me off Scotch and water. By eleven he is imploring me to recite early Yeats and the Shakespeare sonnets to him and his upper lip trembles uninterruptedly, and fat little tears are squeezed out on to his cheeks.

'Repeat that. Repeat it. "That time of year thou mayst in me behold".'

'"When yellow leaves, or none, or few, do hang upon those boughs which shake against the cold"—'

'"Bare ruined choirs, where late the sweet birds *sang*." Isn't that beautiful, beautiful poetry? Come and listen, everybody. Repeat it.'

'You should pack, shouldn't you?'

'You must come and help me pack. And recite some beautiful poems. Will you do that? Will you recite some beautiful poems?'

So Ved and I go back with him to his hotel. When we get up to his room he points to three suitcases.

'That's it. My three beautiful suitcases. My clothes are in the cupboard.'

'We'd better ring for the bearer,' Ved says. We ring, and a slender young man appears.

'Pack this sahib's bags.'

'Bearer!' says the journalist, 'what's your name?'

'Jacob, sir.'

'You're a bloody Christian, Jacob. I bet your father was an untouchable, Jacob.'

'What's he saying?' the bearer asks in Hindi.

'No matter,' Ved says. 'Hurry up with those bags.'

The journalist says, 'Jacob, you have beautiful moustaches, my boy.'

The bearer says, alarmed, 'If the sahib feels like that I can get him the most beautiful girl in India tonight, for a hundred rupees. But I am a family man.'

'Never mind about that,' Ved says. 'Pack quickly.'

Presently the bearer says, 'I have packed two suitcases, sahib.'

'You're a Christian crook, Jacob,' says the journalist. 'Pack the third, you Christian crook.'

'Sahib,' says the bearer, reasonably, 'what with? There is nothing left to pack.'

'That's true,' says the journalist. 'You take the third suitcase, Jacob. Take it and remember me.'

'What is the use of a suitcase to me, sahib?' says the bearer. 'I have nothing to put in it.'

'Okay,' says the journalist. 'Unpack the other two bags.' When the bearer had done that, 'Pack all that stuff in the third bag,' says the journalist, 'and take it away, Jacob. Always be a good Christian.'

'You've got absolutely nothing left,' I protest.

'Jacob's got everything. Jacob likes it, don't you, Jake?'

'Yes, sir,' says the bearer, hastily withdrawing with his bulging suitcase.

'Just a minute,' calls the journalist. 'When will you wear my evening clothes, Jacob?'

'Sir,' says the bearer, 'at weddings and funerals.'

He disappears. It is too late to reason further. Ved and I each carry one empty suitcase downstairs, put them, and with more difficulty the journalist, in the airline bus, and wave goodbye.

Perhaps we should have tried harder to prevent him from parting with his clothes but so passionately misguided a gesture, I thought, had a native charm about it. Also I like the idea of a man who when the Customs asked him if he had anything to declare could answer with perfect and literal truth, 'Nothing.'

Drinks at Narayana's. His wife Rekha, whom I have come to know in the last few days, is there, as beautiful as a fresco from Ajanta. Mala, who has a cold necessitating mustard baths, sits like a cut flower, up to her calves in water, looking wistfully at the veena. Her father's long fingers dwell lightly on it, then move away. He tells me about Husain the painter, who is staying with him and Rekha. Husain came to Bombay as a young man. He was penniless and had to sleep in the streets: to earn a little money he painted people's names on suitcases and umbrellas. Then, one day, he started painting posters for Indian films. He became the most famous poster-painter in the business, earning an enormous salary. He kept it up for a year, then once more abandoned everything and returned to the pavements and the suitcases that needed names painted on. Meanwhile he painted his own pictures, and one day a Bombay art critic saw them and arranged an exhibition. Everything was sold. After that Husain had exhibitions in Paris, Rome, London, Berlin: after Jamini Roy he is perhaps the best-known Indian artist in the West. Now, staying with Narayana, he paints all night: all his new canvases are lined up on one side of the dining-room, as in an exhibition. The dining room smells of unseed oil and paint. Narayana and I stoop, peering into the pictures: some are still wet, they are all thickly painted in whorls, with opaque night-coloured blues and patches of red. Narayana adjusts his spectacles with a delicate forefinger. 'Don't say anything about them when Husain comes. He's very shy.'

In the meantime Han Suyin, the novelist, arrives, a tall and beautiful woman in a Chinese dress with a split skirt; she coils herself into a chair, speaking to nobody save Mala, but watching everybody with an enigmatic curly smile. She has just published a new novel with a Nepalese setting. I ask her what Nepal is like, for I plan to go there. 'Beautiful,' she says, 'but you must go and see, mustn't you? I can't tell you,' and she turns back to Mala.

When Husain comes he turns out to be enormously tall, lean but powerful with grey hair and a thick grey beard. He clasps a tankard of beer in long veined fingers and sits insecurely on a stool beside me. Like Han Suyin, he says nothing, but laughs silently at anything funny that is said. Presently he turns to me and says gently, not looking at me but at a point beyond my left ear, 'I am trying to write poems in English.'

I ask, what about? He replies, 'They are about the same things as my paintings.'

I ask if he will show me some. He withdraws a ragged piece of paper from his pocket and gives it to me. The poem is in rather unskilful free verse, but describes in an extremely precise and graphic manner the flight of a heron, and its manner of landing, dragging its legs for a moment as if it were injured, balancing on its wings.

Just at this moment three other painters burst in, one Krishen Khanna, in a honey-coloured woollen shirt that I immediately covet. He is the most promising of the younger painters. He seems, now, in a gay mood and immediately begins laughing and teasing Husain, who gives me the gentle, hooded smile of one who shares a secret, and replaces the poem in his pocket. For a little while all the room is given up to the newcomers. Krishen Khanna fishes Mala out of her mustard bath and hugs her exuberantly. They talk about prices and sales. When Krishen Khanna comes and sits by me I discover that he is a banker. This surprises me, and seems to surprise him too: as he tells me his eyebrows arch, his mouth goes round and wondering, as if he were Mala listening to one of Ved's Freudian fairy tales.

As the evening wears on Narayana and Han Suyin begin to argue about the Chinese incursions on the border. Narayana keeps saying that the Dalai Lama seems to him a symbol of freedom. Han Suyin disagrees: her eyes flash, she points her finger emphatically as she speaks, as if poking holes in Narayana's argument. The young painters cheer them on. Even Husain takes the opportunity to speak and begins to say something about painting, of which I can catch no more than a few words, for he talks very softly and with his head turned away. Mala, her sneezes reduced to faint protesting sniffs, is bundled off to bed by Rekha. We go on talking till late. I feel happier here than I have yet felt in India: these people are all my friends.

Breakfast with Malcolm MacDonald, the British high commissioner. He was commissioner-general in Southeast Asia before that. I remembered meeting him with my father in Singapore when I was twelve years old. Perhaps adults all seem gigantic to a child: I remember MacDonald being as tall as Stephen Spender, but discovering today that he is actually a small, slightly built man feel nonplussed and as if the basis of conversation has been taken away. But MacDonald is quick to make me easy, he talks about Borneo, Java, the Mekong Valley. As a child I saw some of these places and an interesting game begins, trying to relate ten-year-old memories to MacDonald's descriptions. Things come back: I remember for instance that the Javanese word for Mister is Bung, which used to amuse me greatly at the age of eleven.

A very English breakfast, with scrambled eggs, kidneys, and bacon. I horrify the butler by insisting instead on two raw eggs with tabasco sauce. MacDonald watches me mixing it with interest. 'Can you really eat that?'

'Oh yes, they're frightfully nourishing.'

'I would not eat those,' MacDonald says, 'unless somebody I

was in love with told me to.' He talks about the short stories he has been writing: 'I've been trying to write short stories since I was up at university. I've suppressed all the poetry I wrote then, but I keep the short stories and rework them over and over till I've got nearer to what I want to say.'

He has vivid blue eyes like stains in a bronzed face. Very *simpatico* and full of a nervous energy which one senses will be unleashed the moment breakfast's last kidney has disappeared. I am right: after breakfast, washed down with beer, he gives me a Dutch cigar and takes me on a flying walk round the gardens, pointing to various birds and giving me detailed information about their nesting habits. 'You must know about chaffinches?'

'No,' I say.

'Shame on you. A poet who doesn't know about birds.' He crimps the end of his cigar between his lips and leads me back to the houses, apparently disappointed by my lack of bird-lore.

'What do you think of all this Tibet business going on now?' I venture back in the enormous drawing room filled with Morlands and Sisleys.

He is silent, but presently says, 'The Dalai Lama is in rather a bad position, poor boy. I feel sorry for him. I can't think that anybody would prefer Delhi to Lhasa. Or Mussoorie to Lhasa for that matter.'

'He's coming to Delhi,' I say. 'I'm going to see him.'

'Oh, really? To persuade Nehru to take this business up at the UN no doubt. I wish he had a better chance.'

As I leave, still struggling with my cigar, he seems to think again of the Dalai Lama, and shakes his head. 'Poor boy. I'm sure he'd be happiest at Oxford.'

MacDonald was right: the Indian government has refused to take Tibet's case before the United Nations. They have done this for two reasons: firstly, that neither Tibet nor China is a member of the United Nations; secondly, that Tibet is an internal problem of the Chinese State, in which they do not wish to meddle.

Sophistry, I think: after all India has continually brought up the questions of apartheid in South Africa and French administration in Algeria before the Security Council, and has no more right to meddle in the internal affairs of France and South Africa than in those of China. Also, as Vincent Sheean reminds everybody with an ominous look in his eye, Germany was not a member of the League of Nations when they discussed Hitler's aggression against Poland.

The government is nervous. Chinese troops continue to move about on the border, not frog-stepping, not with caterpillar-footed tanks to tread on dreams of peace, but persuasively, Asiatically, butterfly-hunters with sten-guns. The press carry articles every day—my father is writing one now, scribbling in blue pencil as he does always on large neat sheets of paper—and there have been demonstrations in sympathy with the Tibetans: but a hundred blue pencils and a hundred thousand demonstrators will not remove the nervousness of an entrenched government. Modern politics run so strangely that perhaps that nervousness would only be brushed aside by a newly created nervousness, if an election were at hand.

But then India has nobody else to elect. The last man who seemed likely to be a successor to Nehru was Jayaprakash Narayan. Today Ved and I arrive, a little breathless and late, at a gathering on a terrace, which Jayaprakash Narayan is to address.

He is perhaps the only Indian politician (since Ambedkar, the untouchable leader, died) to have been educated in America. He spent seven years there, and then worked a short while in the Congress under Gandhi before he founded the Indian Socialist Party in 1932. He was then a Marxist Socialist, but drew close to Gandhi in his last years, and after Gandhi's death left the Socialist Party and joined the land-reform movement led by Vinoba Bhave. He has spent the last few years trudging through rivers and across deserts in remote parts of the country getting land for the peasants, more or less in retirement from active politics, but has recently returned to the political scene with a programme of Gandhian Socialism, which is really right-wing Socialism with a Tolstoyan basis.

Jayaprakash Narayan stands at the top of the terrace, looking at about forty people sitting on the ground. He is a man of medium height with a wheat-coloured face, beautiful and deeply lined at the forehead, these lines giving him a curious look of perpetual bewilderment. He wears homespun jodhpurs and an Indian kameez, a shirt that hangs free. He plaits his fingers together, not so much nervously as abstractedly, and considers the crowd.

My father arrives, and takes us up to meet him. With him is Minoo Masani, once a leader of the Socialists under Narayan, who has now transferred allegiance to a new right-wing party, the Swatantra. We have met before, and shake hands. Masani then introduces us.

Jayaprakash Narayan gives us a kindly smile and says something in a voice so soft that I have to strain my ears to catch what he is saying. He pats me on the shoulder and says, 'If you have any questions, please ask them. I won't promise satisfactory answers but I'll do my best.'

As we go back to find places on the terrace my father says, 'J.P. is probably the only politician in India who is an entirely good man.'

'Is he likely to become prime minister?'

'Why not?' Ved asks.

'You'll see in a minute,' says my father.

The first question has been asked. It is about the border situation. Jayaprakash bends his head and considers this in silence. It is quite a long silence. People begin to stir restively. Finally, raising his head, Jayaprakash begins to speak about the government policy. He disagrees with it, he says, but he can see why the government should act as they do. He gives several reasons for this. All governments have to act discreetly, he says. He explains why. It is not boring, partly because a great deal of it is completely inaudible, but partly, too, because he radiates an air of entire honesty, a groping, clumsy honesty that does not mind how much of a fool it makes of itself so long as what is to be said is said. Finally he returns to the point at issue and says that he feels that the borders should be defined more stringently. His answer has taken twenty-five minutes.

The questions go on. So do the answers. At the end the audience dries up and sits in respectful silence. Jayaprakash sighs and asks for a cup of tea. Immediately the audience dissolves: part of it rushes up to Jayaprakash to get his blessing. He is obviously thought of as a saint rather than a politician. I think certainly he is nearer to a saint than he is to a politician. When the crowd has thinned, my father, Ved, and I go up to him.

I ask him about Bhave. He smiles at the name, as though the sound of it made him happy. 'He is somewhere in the Punjab now, I think. The last I heard, he was in a village two hundred miles from Delhi. He seldom comes as close to cities as that. But now he may be five hundred miles from Delhi. He travels quickly, because he travels light.'

He adds, 'On the home front, I think a government that works on Vinobaji's premises is the only feasible one for this country. Of course, Vinobaji himself would not take office in it.'

'Would you take office?'

'I do not seek office.' And again the beautiful and human smile.

I ask about the Dalai Lama. Jayaprakash smiles once more.

'He is our most precious possession at the moment. It is strange that the home of the Dalai Lama should be in our country, though there was one* who made his home here before. But that one was no more than a political refugee. This one is also a symbol of liberty.'

I have heard these words before, from Narayana Menon. Also other words from others. Today the Dalai Lama has come to Delhi, he is staying in Hyderabad House, surrounded by security

---

* The thirteenth Dalai Lama, who fled to Darjeeling in 1910 to escape Manchu rule.

officers, and the drawing rooms chitter and quiver with the latest news about him. A man who saw him coming to Tezpur after his flight from Tibet asserts that there is a halo round his head. Vincent Sheean snorts and says belligerently, 'He's a child.' Marilyn thinks he looks a nice boy. I don't know which is true.

I am to see the Dalai Lama tomorrow.

Kundun

It was raining again. In the gardens of Hyderabad House the lilac-bushes dripped softly; water trickled through the channels of the rockeries and overflowed the normally arid bowls of the fountains. The great house which contained the Dalai Lama stood patiently in the middle distance, being rained on.

I saw all this from outside, through the great gates guarded by Sikh soldiers. Several tents had been pitched on the grass verge of the road to accommodate them and the security officers. A tangle of barbed wire lay, for no apparent purpose, in the grass: the Sikhs came carefully round it as the car drew up at the gate, and asked for my pass.

'I haven't got one.'

'Ha!' one of them said triumphantly. 'Then you cannot enter.'

'I have an appointment.'

'You must see the security officer,' the Sikh said.

So I climbed gingerly out into the rain and was led to a tent where a sad man sat with a telephone at his elbow. He picked this telephone up after I had put my case to him, and gloomily asked it for the private secretary. In a little while the telephone spoke volubly to him. At the end he nodded and put the receiver distastefully back on the hook.

'You are expected. The private secretary will meet you in the entrance. You may not take your car.'

I went back with the soldier who had brought me. He unlocked the gate and let me into the grounds. Then he trotted behind me, extending a small black umbrella that mushroomed from his fist over my head. A second soldier followed carrying the first one's rifle. In this manner, somewhat like a military funeral, we passed down the puddled driveway into the great porch.

A lama in brown robes stood in the porch. He was tall and elderly, and kept his hands in his sleeves. A rosary hung out of one sleeve. He said without pleasure, in English, 'I am the private secretary. Come inside.' We went into the entrance hall. Hyderabad House is now a state guest house, but it was formerly the Delhi palace of the Nizam, and the entrance hall is clearly the entrance hall of a palace: a huge domed roof, marble flooring, and grubby statues everywhere. Several groups of lamas, some in brown robes, some in black, stood talking softly under the dome that filtered a submarine light into the hall beneath. Their rosaries clicked softly. The private secretary deposited me on a sofa and went swimming away from me with prodigious strides, his robes floating about him. A young lama approached and sat, a little shyly, at my side.

He asked, in excellent English, if I had come to see His Holiness. Yes, I said. Was I a journalist? I denied this. He suddenly laughed and shook a finger at me: 'Ah, I see it, you are a poet. I see it by your hair.' To change the subject I asked him where he had learnt his English. He had been to school in India, he said.

'Then this isn't your first visit?'

'No, indeed, but I hope it will be the last.'

'Why?' He shrugged and wouldn't answer.

I asked him if he had come out with the Dalai Lama. He said yes. 'That was a terrible trip,' he said, 'a terrible trip. I do not like to remember.'

At this point the private secretary came hurrying back with a harassed-looking Indian official and a slender young Sikkimese in a bush shirt. The lama beside me vanished, and the official sat down in his place and said emphatically: 'You understand that the condition on which this audience has been granted is that you should ask no political questions?' I nodded. 'Please keep to that condition. Now, there are certain other things. Do not touch His Holiness. That is sacrilege. When the audience is terminated, do not turn your back on His Holiness. Leave the room backwards. Also, kindly do not ask His Holiness rude questions.'

'How do you mean, rude questions?'

'Do not ask His Holiness if he believes that he is a god.'

'It had never occurred to me to do so,' I said truthfully.

'Very well.' He beckoned to the Sikkimese. 'This gentleman is your interpreter. Please remember that he will not translate political questions. His Holiness will now receive you.'

The interpreter led me out of the entrance hall through a carpeted corridor that emerged on a square courtyard. This courtyard had taken on the air of a lamasery already: groups of lamas stood about talking, as in the entrance hall, and two or three sat on rugs turning prayer-wheels. The drone of their prayers came to me through the rain-cooled air. The interpreter paused at a doorway on one side of the courtyard, whispering to me, 'Prepare yourself.' Then he turned into the room, and I followed.

It was a big drawing room, full of sofas and occasional tables, and looking over the garden. In the middle of acres of carpet the Dalai Lama stood smiling. From his photographs I had always got the impression of somebody with an elongated body and enormous head: I was surprised to find him actually a sturdy, broad-shouldered, tall young man. He had clear skin and rosy cheeks, and wore black-rimmed pince-nez, slightly inappropriate-looking on the young face. His brown robe was open at the neck to reveal a tan shirt. He came forward and gave me an extremely firm handshake. The interpreter fluttered and kept trying to entice us to various sofas. Finally the Dalai Lama chose one by the window, pointed firmly to it, and turned to me, smiling. He gestured and said in English, 'Please sit.'

It was an enormous sofa. I sank into it with trepidation. The Dalai Lama sat beside me and the interpreter drew up a chair facing us. The Dalai Lama crossed his legs composedly, revealing under the robe brown brogues and a pair of red socks with yellow stripes. He spoke first. His voice was deep and clear, and he spoke rather fast, giving an impression of tremendous eagerness. He spoke in Tibetan, but looked at me all the while with brown intelligent eyes.

'His Holiness would much like to read some of your poetries,' said me interpreter. 'Is it possible for you to send him some poetries?'

'Yes, certainly. Has His Holiness read a great deal of literature then, apart from Tibetan literature?'

This was translated, and the Dalai Lama shook his head emphatically, the corners of his mouth turned down in a charming and rueful smile. I felt this was an answer, and was surprised when the interpreter began, rather hurriedly, to translate:

'His Holiness is familiar with all the literatures of the world.'

I asked, ignoring this fatuity, 'Is there any secular literature in Tibet? The recent revolt, for instance, did that produce any literature?'

The interpreter translated this. He addressed the Dalai Lama as 'Kundun', his usual Tibetan title, which means 'Presence'. As he ended each sentence he sketched a little obeisance with hand and head. Kundun thought carefully, and then answered.

'His Holiness says that he does not know of any literature, but there may be some. The difficulty about finding out would be that such literature manuscripts will be in Tibet and not India.'

'If they could be found I would like to try and translate them, if His Holiness feels that their publication in the West would help the Tibetan cause.'

The Dalai Lama nodded when this was translated, and smiled with his vivid smile. He leant forward, tapped me on the knee, and said something. 'His Holiness thanks you for your interest in the Tibetan people. He hopes to be able to send some of the young men of his people to your university, to Oxford, and to other Western universities. He will see if he is able to afford, and if possible he will send.'

'Does His Holiness not feel that young men brought up in an exclusively Eastern society in Tibet may have difficulty in the West?'

The Dalai Lama surprisingly began to answer this before it was translated. He shook his head emphatically at the start, then went on, talking quickly with many gestures of one long, capable hand, and occasionally reaching over to tap me on the knee. He smiled all the while, but usually a little wryly, the corners of his mouth turned down; it was only when he was genuinely amused or interested that the corners of the mouth lifted, the cheeks got pinker, and the eyes gleamed. Now he was explaining something unpleasant, and the smile was downturned.

'His Holiness says that the Chinese have already altered the structure of Tibetan society and introduced Western things. They have done this by force and brutality but they have altered Tibet in a way that has made it impossible for Tibetans to return entirely to their old system. Tibet will have to turn more and more to the West.'

I recalled the Dalai Lama's flight from Lhasa. 'When His Holiness left the Potala, we were told there was a great dust storm that prevented the Chinese from seeing him. Some people have suggested that this dust storm was sent by Providence. Does His Holiness agree?'

His Holiness shrugged his shoulders, and said something.

'Kundun says that there are many dust storms in Tibet at that season.'

I laughed at this. The Dalai Lama laughed too and again tapped me gently on the knee. 'How did His Holiness feel during the flight?'

This was answered briefly: 'Nervous.'

'Can His Holiness remember his childhood before he was chosen as the Dalai Lama?'

The Dalai Lama nodded.

'Does he have any clear memories of it? Did he feel any different to other children?'

The Dalai Lama looked thoughtful at this. The long hands moved as though sketching a childhood in the air. But he shook his head.

'His Holiness has no particular memory of that part of his life. He cannot tell if he felt any different from other children, because he had no standards of comparison. But his mother always said that he was the noisiest child she had ever seen.'

The Dalai Lama watched me closely throughout the translation. When the interpreter reached the last sentence, an expectant gleam came into his eyes, and when I laughed he joined delightedly in the laughter. He leant forward and said something to the interpreter.

'Kundun asks if you have any more questions.'

'Not if he doesn't want any more.'

The Dalai Lama looked pleased when this was translated. He smiled, rubbed his hands together boyishly, and spoke again to the interpreter.

'His Holiness says it is good that you have no more questions because now you can both talk properly. He says he is sorry he does not speak English, he is learning, but as yet he cannot speak it well. He asks you what you studied at Oxford.'

I said literature. The Dalai Lama nodded. The next question was about the methods of instruction. I explained the tutorial system. Again he nodded.

'Kundun thinks this is a good method. He asks you to describe the life in Oxford.'

So I found myself explaining scouts, landladies, the importance of the pub, the bicycle, and the river. The Dalai Lama listened to all this closely, occasionally stopping me to put in various questions. What was a punt? What academic dress did people wear? Why were colleges locked at midnight? Finally he made a quick switch of topic.

'Kundun wishes to know to how many countries you have been?'

And, after I had given him a list, 'How many languages can you speak?' As this was translated the Dalai Lama leant across to me and interjected inquiringly: 'Spanish?'

I shook my head. 'French, Italian, a little German, a little Greek.'

The Dalai Lama, seeming disappointed, asked again, 'Spanish-no?'

'Tell His Holiness I can't speak Spanish. Why is he so interested in Spanish?'

'He has seen a book of pictures about Spain. It seems to him a very beautiful country. He wishes that he could visit Oxford and travel to European countries, especially to Spain.'

'Does he plan to travel a lot?'

The Dalai Lama for the first time looked sad. His hands lay inert in his lap as he spoke. 'Kundun says that he cannot be interested in travel except in so far as it will help his country. He may visit some of the Buddhist countries, and if the Tibetan case is brought before the UN he may go to America, but he will always make India his base, and always return to it, because it is near his country.'

The Dalai Lama now spoke again, slowly and sadly. His face was grim, shadowed, quiet. He spoke for a long time. When he had finished the interpreter looked nervous.

'I cannot translate that.'

The Dalai Lama leant across again, putting his hand on my knee, and spoke urgently and even a little imperiously to the interpreter, who shook his head respectfully. He was sorry, he could not translate. I was divided between irritation and nervousness: nervousness because I was sure that in allowing the Dalai Lama to tap me on the knee, I was committing some awful unconscious sacrilege. I kept edging unobtrusively away, but he had obligingly humped himself along in my wake, so that by now we had traversed the entire length of the sofa and I was more or less pinioned against the farther arm. I hoped no lamas would look in. There was not much of my thought left free for me to feel irritated with, but I managed.

'Can't you just give me the gist of what His Holiness is saying?'

And then suddenly, coldly, precisely, the Dalai Lama lifted his voice. He spoke only a few words, but the interpreter looked up into his face and hurriedly began to translate.

'Kundun says that there are many people not far from here who speak of peace, truth, and goodwill. They are constantly lecturing others about this. They make promises in the name of peace and goodwill, yet when the time comes to keep those promises, they are always broken. This is as great a danger as aggressive militarism, in a different way.'

He hesitated.

'Kundun says there are two great forces in the world today. One is the force of the people with power, with armies to enforce their power, and with a land to recruit their armies from. The other is the force of the poor and dispossessed. The two are in perpetual conflict, and it is certain who will lose.'

The Dalai Lama added something to this. The interpreter again hesitated, but catching the Dalai Lama's eye stumbled on into a very curious remark.

'His Holiness says that this is the reason why there are so many suicides in the world today.'

There was a silence. The Dalai Lama's grave, stooped face did not change. I said rather lamely, 'That is quite true.'

The Dalai Lama spoke again. The interpreter said, 'Unless this is changed, the world will perish, Kundun says. Therefore every poet, every religious man, every political leader, should fight against this division till he dies. The teachings of the Lord Buddha also tell us this.'

'How does he think poets should do this?'

The Dalai Lama launched into a long, obviously detailed answer. He emphasized each point with a tap on my knee. His forehead wrinkled a little with concentration.

When he had finished, I asked, 'What did Kundun say?'

The interpreter, looking baffled, replied, 'He says poets must insert references to Tibet in their poems.'

The Dalai Lama shook his head helplessly at me, and suddenly laughed. We both laughed together once more, which was nice. I realized that I had been there for more than an hour, and that I should go. We all stood up and the Dalai Lama dropped his arm round my shoulders in a friendly gesture. He came quite close. I saw that the Dalai Lama has freckles on his nose.

He shook my hand with the same firm clasp as before, and stepped aside. I remembered what I had been told about not turning my back. I accordingly began to sidle out backward, crab-fashion. The Dalai Lama watched me for a moment. Then he suddenly took a few steps forward, dropped his hands to my shoulders, and turned me round so that I faced the door. He gave me a friendly push to speed me on my way. I heard his laugh behind me, for the last time.

Outside the door the grim black-robed elder lamas were standing, rosaries in their gnarled fingers. I looked back. Kundun was standing alone in the middle of the room as he had done when I came in. I waved at him across all those acres of carpet. He waved back, and briefly, the beautiful smile came again to his face.

Then I went away.

Ved had decided to come to Nepal with me. My father arranged that we should stay with a Nepalese general of his acquaintance. He armed me with introductions to the general and to Mr Gupta, his correspondent there, and the day after I had seen the Dalai Lama Ved and I left for Patna, en route to Kathmandu.

Living Like a Rana

From Patna we flew for an hour across the yellow flood-smudged plains of Bihar. Ved slept phlegmatically at my side, and I took surreptitious pulls at my hip-flask, avoiding the cold eye of the air hostess. Then the Heron began to flounder among clouds, and knobbly forested hills appeared below. The hills matured and became mountains: the Heron mountain-hopped, sailing between two scarred peaks, rising to miss a third, dropping between two more, and Ved awoke amidst the bounces. 'What in hell is happening now, Dommie?'

'Mountains,' I said. 'We must be nearly there.'

We were, for the Heron skipped neatly over a final peak, and slanted down to the Kathmandu Valley.

We landed on a narrow brown airstrip, with slate-coloured buffaloes scattering along the runway as the Heron came down. When we climbed out the sun hit us: a gross sun looking from the exact centre of the sky, frizzling the grass.

'For a seasoned traveller,' Ved said, 'your information is a bit unreliable. I thought you said it would be freezing in Nepal.'

'I thought it might be,' I said humbly, and we walked to the Customs building.

We were clearing our luggage when Mr Gupta came up. He was small and plump, in a brown suit, and he said, 'Mr Mehta and Mr Moraes?'

'Yes.'

'Your plane is very late. The general sahib came yesterday, he came today, but you did not come. Now he has gone to Parliament, but he has left you his car.'

We cleared our luggage, and Mr Gupta showed us to the general's car.

'I will see you later,' Mr Gupta said. 'You will be very comfortable in the palace.'

As we drove away, Ved said, 'What did he mean, the palace? We're not staying with the king, are we?'

'Well,' I said, 'this general probably lives in a palace.'

'This,' said Ved, 'is going to be quite something, Dommie.'

The Kathmandu Valley is very flat, but it is ringed round by mountains. It was these mountains, enormous and thickly forested, their shadows slanting into the lowlands, that were the first things one noticed, and we never got away from them. Wherever you go in Nepal the mountains come with you, in shadow or in substance: the eastern Himalayas; and away to the north, the Everest.

The valley is cultivated, mostly: the peasants grow rice, maize, and beans, buffaloes pull the carved wooden ploughs in the narrow acres, and everywhere the bearded speargrass waves in the wind, and red hibiscus coils suddenly out of the trees. We passed through three or four villages on the way into Kathmandu: Nepalese women, full-breasted and brown, dressed in tunics and skirts, pounded maize before every door, and the doors were as beautiful as they: very old, wooden, carved intricately, rather meaninglessly, but intricately; now and then they leant open and children fell squalling into each dirty street.

It took us about half an hour to reach the palace.

We reached it by turning off the main road and scrambling a hundred yards up a dirt track. People sat on each side of the track, mostly women, with cloths spread before them on the ground, covered with red peppers and speargrass drying in the sun. As we passed, they rose, making deep obeisance, unsmilingly respectful. I told Ved.

'They must be very polite people in Nepal,' Ved said.

'It's probably only that we are in the general's car.'

We drove through wrought-iron gates, shushed over a gravel drive winding through ornamental gardens, and arrived at the palace. It was a huge, ugly building, four storeys high, uncompromising in the green September, the Himalayas behind it.

The driver turned to us. 'The palace of the Rana,' he said.

Two servants met us in the high entrance hall of the palace. They took our bags, and led us through a courtyard to a flight of stairs. Then we climbed four floors, through winding corridors and anterooms, to a long gallery with rooms leading off it. All the corridors were hung with framed illustrations from *Picture Post, Titbits*, and so on, alternating with the heads of assassinated tigers, glaring soulfully through glass eyes, and photographs of dead Ranas, tiger-whiskered, soulful-eyed, clutching their jewelled swords. The servants showed us into a sitting room off the gallery. The gallery was obviously part of the general's own quarters; the sitting room was festooned in the same way as the corridors had been, and furnished with huge overstuffed chairs, elephant's-foot ashtrays, and beautifully carved Nepalese tables. Presents from Clacton stood on the tables. The tigers leered inexhaustibly from the walls. We sank into a sofa and the servants disappeared. We heard voices in the distance.

'I expect someone will come for us,' I said.

'Coo, Dommie!' Ved said, 'this really is a palace.'

At this point I became aware of an enormous Himalayan bear crouched next to the sofa. It glowered at me. I gasped.

'Now what is it?'

'There is a bear next to us. It must,' I added, groping for common sense, 'be stuffed.'

'Honestly, Dommie, I know you have a fantasy life, but what do you think? Have you ever known anybody who kept a live bear in their drawing room?'

'I only wondered,' I was beginning lamely, when the bear rose, snarled at us, and shambled loosely out through the farther door.

I was saved from the necessity of comment by the appearance of a plump, handsome lady in a sari. She floated toward us, smiling and making the namaskar. We introduced ourselves and she sat by us, smiling still. She was the general's wife, and she spoke only Hindi. In fact she was Indian, from the Kangra Valley, for the Ranas from time immemorial have married in India in order to keep the Rana blood uncontaminated.

I had picked up a little Hindi, by now, and was not as embarrassed as I might have been. Ved filled in my gaps.

'You look very much like your father,' said the Rani; she had a very soft, calming, dreaming voice, and I even forgot the bear for a few minutes. Then I felt I should mention it.

'There was a bear here a few minutes ago,' I said, feeling idiotic.

'Ah yes,' said the Rani dreamily. 'Which bear?'

'You have several?'

'Oh yes. That is one thing you must be careful about: don't go out at night; they don't see very well in the dark, and they might not know you were guests.'

And then, smiling, 'Would you like some tea? And then a bath? I know what boys are.'

It was very soothing. 'I will send my son in to see you,' she said. 'He is your age.'

The son came in a few minutes later. He was thin, pale, and bespectacled; he wore jodhpurs and a long coat, and on his head a bucket-shaped cloth hat.

'You are poets,' he said.

'Mr Moraes is,' said Ved. 'So he frequently tells me.'

'That is good, I too am a poet.' He paused and beamed.

We remained silent, so he went on, 'The best in Nepal, except for Devkota of course.' After another short silence, he continued, 'That is because I am the only poet of high birth: I am the only poet who is a Rana.'

'What are your poems about?' Ved asked.

'They are about the struggles of the poor. I am very liberal-minded, you see.'

The Rani brought in the tea. We drank it in silence.

Finally the poet said: 'You are here for long?'

'Oh, fairly long,' I replied.

'Excellent! I shall read my poems to you frequently in the evenings. It will help to pass your time.'

We finished our tea. 'Poor boys,' the Rani said, 'you must be tired. Your servant will take you to your room. Pannalal!' she called. A lean sulky Nepalese appeared and the Rani handed us over to him.

Our room was one floor up, at the top. It was a sort of hall, furnished with two vast mosquito-curtained beds. The walls were entirely covered with photographs of dead whiskery Ranas. Pannalal stood by the door, hands folded.

'The dining room is next door,' he said. 'You will take your breakfast there.'

'All right,' I said.

He remained where he was.

'It's all right,' I said. 'We don't need you.'

'I am your servant,' he said. 'I will stay here. You may need me suddenly.'

Suddenly there were footsteps on the stairs. The poet appeared.

'Is everything all right?' he said. 'If this dog here does not serve you properly, beat him. My father will see you for dinner at seven-thirty.'

He nodded, and went away. A minute later he came back.

'I have written four new poems today. I am very prolific. I have nothing to do all day, and I find poetry a good pastime. Shall I come before dinner and read them to you?'

'That would be a great pleasure,' Ved said limply.

The poet departed. Pannalal remained.

I fished the whisky out of my suitcase. 'I think we need a drink.'

'Yes,' Ved said.

We drank in silence, under Pannalal's eye. Then Ved said, 'It's an odd prospect.'

'Yes,' I said.

They were the last feudal overlords that the world has seen, these Ranas. Originally Indian princelings, they crossed the high passes into Nepal hundreds of years ago, and established themselves as the ruling class. The king still sat in Kathmandu, but the Ranas pulled the strings, and he danced for them. All over Kathmandu they built their fantastic palaces, where they lived, bearded pard men in jewelled robes, surrounded by the women they had abducted from their families, with the power of life and death over any Nepalese who was not a Rana. When one of them passed, any ordinary citizen who failed to do obeisance till he was out of sight was thrown into gaol. As late as 1942 the chief Rana used to ride an elephant through the streets of Kathmandu every month. The women of the town were required to stand outside their houses, and whichever took the Rana's fancy were immediately seized by his soldiers and taken to his harem. If husbands or fathers bothered the Rana thereafter they were gaoled. One village, Halembu, in the mountains, renowned for its beautiful women, was raided and the entire female population taken off to the harems.

One reason for this abounding appetite was probably that the Ranas were bored: they had nothing to do but copulate. One result of it was that over the years three distinct grades of Rana emerged: first-class Ranas, born of a legal wife, second-class Ranas, the sons of established mistresses, and third-class Ranas, the unfortunate result of slips that passed in the night. Every Rana, however, whatever class he belongs to, is born with the rank of a general. He is also born with a name: Shumshere Jung Bahadur Rana.

Nepal is an independent state. It has been invaded, but not often. For one thing, it was always difficult to get to the Kathmandu Valley, which is sealed in by mountains: Tibet to the north, Sikkim to the east, Bengal to the south, and Kumaon westward. The Gurkhas were the most successful of the invaders: they conquered and occupied the country in 1768, but in due course eddied away into the stream of Nepalese life and became one of the races of the country. Later, the Nepalese signed treaties with the British, and helped them during the Indian Mutiny and the First World War, supplying them with men, and, rather inexplicably, cardamoms.

Contact with the West had a strange effect on the Ranas. The British officers who visited Kathmandu brought whisky and soda in their mule-trains, and apparently offered it to the Ranas, who drank it, but seem to have felt a little irked at having been outdone. Accordingly they sent emissaries over the mountains to India; and next time the British came, they were offered a drink that put their plebeian beverage to shame. It was whisky and champagne. Excessive consumption of this elixir may explain why most of the Ranas in the nineteenth century died before forty.

The Ranas did everything in a big way. One of the sons of the house where we stayed told me of the time when his father wanted to send him to Eton. To finance the trip they had to approach the head of the family, the grandfather, a Rana of the Ranas. On being told of the project, he flew into a rage.

'No grandson of mine will be permitted to defile himself by crossing the black waters to England,' he said furiously. 'But I will be reasonable. If you like, you may hire all the masters from Eton and bring them here.'

Later, the grandfather fell ill. A British surgeon was fetched from India. When he arrived, he discovered that the old man's palace was on top of an unroaded hill; he could not imagine how he was to get his equipment up. He went to bed that night, still in a quandary, in a tent at the foot of the hill. He awoke next morning to find a road leading from the door of his tent up to the gate of the palace. It had been built in six hours by relays of slave-gangs working through the night.

So the Ranas lived on in their mad palaces, drinking their invented drink, begetting hundreds of children, taxing the men of Nepal and kidnapping the women, until 1951. In that year the Nepalese rose. The Ranas tried to seize the king, who fled to Delhi. They were overthrown. Most of them left the country and settled in Bangalore, a kind of Indian Cheltenham. There they still moulder, seedy old generals planning revolution over glasses of orange juice. The Nepalese Congress took over government and drafted a constitution. Elections were held in 1958, and the Congress, under the youthful B.P. Koirala, came in again with a crushing majority. It is a Socialist party, and such Ranas as remain in Kathmandu are now taxed for the first time in recorded history.

They were also required, in 1951, to cut down on their concubines (some houses had as many as seven hundred) and ordered to reduce this number by two-thirds. As a natural result, on the day when the order was executed, the streets of Kathmandu were filled by hundreds of loudly lamenting women with nowhere to go. Koirala solved the problem very resourcefully by marrying them off to the Assam Riflemen who had come in from India to help him keep the peace.

The peace has been kept so far. Though Nepal is a sovereign state, it relies heavily on India for aid, in road-building, for instance, and the training of troops. The Nepalese extremists have accused Nehru of colonialist designs on their country, but I think his interest is purely avuncular. Moreover India is interested in strengthening Nepal, for Nepal lies between India and Tibet, and in Tibet are the Chinese.

We were drinking rather gloomily when a plump young man in spectacles, with a round smooth smiling face, bounced in. Pannalal promptly fell to the floor, kissing his feet. The young man looked embarrassed.

'Get up, get up,' he said, and to us, 'I'm the general's second son, his engineer son. I came to see how you were getting on.'

'Oh, fine,' we said, and he laughed.

'You mean you're bored? Me too. Can I have a drink?'

'Do,' I said, and poured one.

'I thought,' said the engineer son, rapidly draining his glass, 'that you might like to have a peep round the palace.'

'We would indeed,' I said.

'It's very large,' said Ved doubtfully.

'Five hundred rooms. Don't worry, we won't go round them all. They're mostly full of pictures of my ancestors. We could have a look at the courtyard and the grounds.'

'Good,' I said, 'but have another drink.'

We had finished the bottle by the time we rose, and the engineer son was more expansive than ever. He led us down to the ground floor. It was a long way.

'Who lives in these five hundred rooms?'

'Well, my father has five of us, you know. Five sons. We each have quarters for ourselves and our families. Then lots of the rooms are guest rooms, drawing rooms, that kind of thing. And of course the maidservants have one wing.'

'Maidservants?' inquired Ved. The engineer son laughed and inserted an elbow into Ved's ribs. 'We had more of them before 1951, of course. About two hundred and fifty. Now I think the actual number is about a hundred and fifty. Useful girls, they do everything, ha, ha!' The elbow drove into my ribs this time.

We went out through a carved wooden porch into the main courtyard. The palace was rectangular and the courtyard a rectangle within a rectangle. It was very busy: men and women in loose tunics and felt shoes moved ceaselessly through it—the servants: the women almost all young and pretty. And on three sides of the courtyard there were shops. There were a blacksmith and a goldsmith, a cobbler, a tailor, a barber, a dispensary, and, in one corner, an anonymous doorway to which the engineer son pointed.

'That's the most important of all. The bank.'

He nudged Ved again, laughing.

'Who uses these shops?'

He looked at me, surprised. 'Why, we do. The family. We pay all these people, and they serve us.'

'What's the idea?' Ved said.

'When these palaces were built the Ranas had the idea of setting up autonomous communities in each one. All these people live in our house, and we take care of them. We feed and clothe them, and they serve us. It is like a little city. We even have a school in the grounds, for their children.'

'And are all the Rana's palaces like this?'

'They were,' said the engineer son. 'This is one of the last ones left. Things are changing. It was all very well, but the kind of life we led couldn't have gone on much longer: after all, not so long ago, I would have had the power of life and death over most of these people. It's a good thing,' he added surprisingly, 'that that's all over.'

We moved back through the house into the gardens outside. It was getting dark, and mist came bubbling gently in from the mountains. The engineer son shrugged.

'We'll have to see the grounds some other time. But I'll point a few things out. The stables and the dairies are over there. And the vegetable gardens. The fruit gardens are on the other side of the house. We keep the livestock beyond the stables: they have their paddocks there. Sometime I must show you our pigs; they are the best in Nepal.'

He said, 'We'll have to give it all up in a few years. The taxation is going up under Koirala.'

'Don't you regret it?' Ved said.

'No. I was a boy when the whole thing changed. I've grown up with it. It's the older people who find it difficult. You'll meet some this evening. Meanwhile, why not come up to my sitting room and have a drink?'

'A pleasure,' we said.

We dined with the general. He was a youngish fifty, and looked very much like his engineer son, except that he wore delicate gold-rimmed pince-nez. He made us a small effusive speech of welcome, but then said nothing: it was obvious that he didn't quite know what to do with us. In the uncomfortable hour after dinner he kept plunging across to one or the other of us, fetching a drink, a cigarette, or an ashtray: he would give it to one, stare searchingly into one's face, his lips rounding as if in surprise, and then plunge back across the room. The poet son sat sulkily quiet, annoyed because we hadn't been there to listen to his poems; the engineer son maintained a discreet silence; there was a third son, who had been at Sandhurst, who talked about shooting, and he was the only one who did talk. The Rani fussed over Ved and me, murmuring like a dove: now and then she asked us if we had any brothers or sisters. That was all, except for a very old Rana, a field marshal who sat hunched in a chair all through the evening. He was small, with a round starch-coloured face, the lips puckered in with age; he kept his tiny slippered feet together; his hands, dry leaves, lay together in his lap; He ate and drank with an almost inconspicuous flutter of hand to mouth, a sudden ingestion of the lips: after dinner he smoked, delicately, a cigar. He did not speak at all, except once. Ved was trying to draw the general out on some question of Nepalese politics, the general being a Member of Parliament, and Ved was not succeeding. Finally with a courteous little Oxford swivel of attention, he turned to the field marshal.

'What do *you* think, sir?'

The field marshal said in a high crackling voice: 'I wish the days were back when we chased the peasants through the streets with *whips!'* Then his face became once more starched and impassive, only he kept sucking in his lips after his remark, as though it had made him thirsty.

It was not a very successful dinner.

When we said goodnight, the general drew himself up, looked

over our heads, and said rapidly, 'I hope I have not forgotten anything that would make you comfortable.'

'Oh no, sir,' we said.

The engineer son winked at us and said softly, 'One for the road.'

'What a good idea,' Ved said, and we followed the drink-giver.

When, at about midnight, we stumbled back to our room, we found Pannalal asleep across the doorway. We stepped over him. 'Do you want the light, Dommie?'

'No,' I said.

We undressed in the dark. Ved was quicker than I was. He moved over to his bed while I was still fastening my pyjama trousers. I heard him struggling through the mosquito-curtain, and then came a yell of horror.

My first thought was of stray bears. I rushed to the light-switch and turned it on. Ved was scrambling out of his bed, which now contained a very pretty Nepalese girl. She didn't have any clothes on. When I turned to my bed, there was one there too. She laughed and made an unmistakable gesture.

Pannalal had now woken up. He stood doomfully in the door, wiping the sleep out of his eyes.

'What are these girls doing here?' I said.

'The general sahib sent them to entertain you. If they are not pretty enough I will fetch two others.'

'No, no,' I said, and cravenly retired into the dining room, leaving Ved to cope with the situation.

When I returned the girls had gone. Pannalal, looking very indignant, was going back to sleep.

'How did you get rid of them?' I asked admiringly.

'I said we both had a contagious disease.'

'Genius,' I said.

'Just a knack, just a knack, nothing at all,' Ved said, crawling back through the mosquito-curtain. 'Poof, they use very strong scent.'

He added, 'Apart from our other responsibilities, Dommikins, there are *two* of us in this damned room, after all.'

'Not to mention Pannalal.'

'Not to mention Pannalal. I don't think they believed me, you know. They'll probably think we are queer, and send us two menservants tomorrow.'

Several Priests

The general came up next morning as we were finishing breakfast brooded over by Pannalal. He polished one hand nervously with the other and said: 'How are you?'

Ved said, 'Very well, thank you, sir,' while I wondered how someone who had had so much power could be so shy.

'Everything is to your satisfaction?' inquired the general, like a hotel manager, and again Ved, who had just been complaining bitterly about the lavatory, said yes, splendid.

'I hope,' said the General, 'that the wolfhounds did not disturb you in the night. They are Tibetan wolfhounds, very fierce, which we keep in the grounds, and generally they howl at night.'

'No,' I said, 'everything was fine.'

Then the general gave a conspiratorial smile. 'I hear,' he said, 'that you are ill.'

'Ill?' I said, and then remembered Ved's alibi and nodded vigorously.

The general actually giggled. 'Fine!' he said. 'I am always telling my sons that nobody becomes a man till they have had a dose.'

Ved, who did not quite get what he meant, said, 'Of what?' and I produced a knowing smile.

'Don't worry about it,' advised the general. 'You will find your powers have increased when it is over.'

And he toddled off, rubbing his hands together with real satisfaction. 'What was all that about?' inquired Ved.

'Your contagious disease,' I said. 'They think we have the clap.'

'Good God!' said Ved puritanically.

'It was a fairly natural conclusion for them to draw,' I pointed out. 'Besides, our prestige has obviously gone up.'

'Except with Pannalal,' Ved said gloomily. 'Did you hear what the general said? They have bears in the drawing room and wolves in the garden.'

'Wolfhounds,' I corrected.

'And concubines in the beds. And, Dommie, the lavatory is awful. And I have the colic, Dommie. The colic!'

'Every cloud,' I said, 'has its silver lining.'

We went, in a jeep-taxi, to the airlines office. It is in the main street, the Jyuddha. This is a narrow frontier-town area meandered through by fleets of pedestrians and bicyclists, leading at one end into the green acreage of the Parade Ground, said to be the largest in the world, and at the other into the teeming market of the old town. We were confirming our reservations for Calcutta when a young Indian came up to Ved.

'Excuse me if I am forward: but are you Mr Ved Mehta?'

'Yes,' said Ved while I thought cynically how depressing it was to see him so exhilarated to be recognized in Kathmandu.

'I thought I recognized you from your pictures. And can this possibly be Mr Dom Moraes?'

I was overjoyed. 'Delighted to see you,' I said cordially.

'I am a professor of literature, one of the Indian professors loaned to the Nepal government. I heard that you were coming. A coincidence that I should run into you!'

'Come and have a drink,' I said automatically.

'I will do that when I come to England. You must come and drink with me.'

'Far from here?' asked Ved, who hates walking.

'Not so far. Two furlongs.'

'We'd love to,' I said.

We walked through the Jyuddha into the market. Here everything grew more congested. Wooden and brick houses, two storey tall, huddled into the roadway. We passed a temple of carved stone, outside which an enormous wooden chariot, thirty feet high, stood.

'That is the juggernaut,' said the professor. 'The chariot of the god. When the festival comes and the chariot is drawn through Kathmandu, they have to take down the telephone wires to give it free passage.'

We came to a narrow, cluttered street, which smelt of a lack of drains. 'This is the middle-class residential area,' the professor said, 'where I live.'

Children defecated in the middle of the road, dogs snuffed languorously at patches of old excrement, cows moaned in their dewlaps and ambled past. At intervals a rubbish heap spilled across the street and one had to climb over. Scattered over and around each rubbish heap, like lumps of grey wool flecked with blood, were the corpses of many rats.

'There was recently a cholera epidemic in Kathmandu,' the professor said.

The women and children looked rosy and healthy. They screamed at each other up and down the street, the mothers pounding their maize and drying their peppers by the fly-steaming rubbish heaps and in the carved wooden doorways. At length we reached the extreme end of the street. The professor led us through a gateway into a compound, a patch of grass with a few ragged daisies. Somebody had been using the entrance to the house as a lavatory. We negotiated the mess and climbed two flights of extremely narrow and circuitous wooden stairs to the two rooms where he lived with his wife, two children, younger brother, and sister-in-law.

In the main room there were a sofa, a table, and three chairs. Somebody had hung a reproduction of the 'Mona Lisa' on one wall, upside down. A few textbooks lay on the table, and some

Green Penguins in a corner. We sat down on the sofa. I felt a little uneasy, for the professor seemed suddenly depressed; he sank heavily into a chair, sighing, rubbing his face with his hands, and I was afraid he would think we despised him for the way in which he had to live. He had a sad and gentle face, with a little moustache, which he twisted uneasily between his fingers. His wife came out, her sari over her head, and squatted on the floor, not looking at us. The two children appeared with streaming noses, and the brother and his wife came silently to the two vacant chairs.

'Not like England, eh?' said the professor with a sad little laugh.

'It's charming,' I said. It must be difficult to find places in Kathmandu.'

'Ah, when a man marries, he can say goodbye to comfort,' the professor said.

He went into the other room and returned with a bottle of Rémy Martin. As he returned a rat scurried across the room, and he kicked angrily at it. His brother got up silently and fetched three glasses.

For a minute everybody was like a ghost. The room had power over us, silencing us all. Then Ved said, 'What very good brandy.'

The professor began to unlock his floodgates. 'You have no idea,' he said bitterly, '—how can you have any idea?—how badly paid we teachers are in India. Even I—I come here from the Indian government and I get paid just enough to keep myself and this, my family. You can have no idea,' he kept repeating, shaking his head.

Then suddenly he looked up and laughed charmingly. 'I am being foolish,' he said. 'Drink up your brandy and have another. Now, is there anything I can do to help you while you are in Nepal?'

'It would be nice to meet some students,' Ved said.

'That is a good idea. The Nepalese students, believe it or not, are far better than Indian students. They have more sense of discipline, and they are intellectually livelier. They ask questions.

My God, you have no idea what a relief it is to have students who ask questions! Also the girls in Nepal are much freer than Indian girls: you will notice that there is no inequality of the sexes in Nepal: the women talk freely, and they are interested in the outside world, and a far higher percentage of girls come to university here than in India.'

'There is a university, then?'

'Not as yet. They are building one near Kirtipur. As yet there are only colleges, and few of those. There are not enough teachers, you see. But already they have started giving the brighter boys scholarships to go abroad, to America and England, and so they are preparing the way. Those boys will come back to teach.'

'You find the students enthusiastic then?' Ved said.

'Oh yes. That can be proved by the fact that most of them have outside jobs, as clerks and stenographers in some of the embassies, and they come to college at odd hours, some even in the night. They are good students,' said the professor.

'It is all a result of these Ranas,' he added. 'While they were in power, they usually denied education to the masses because they were afraid that it might be dangerous. Now that it is possible to be educated, everybody wants it. The Ranas have always thrown boomerangs. All their little despotisms come back and knock them unconscious. It's impossible that they could ever return to power in Nepal.'

'We're staying with some,' I said.

'Ah, so? Which ones?'

We told him, and Ved launched into his grievance about lavatories.

'But, my good friend, you must not expect lavatories in a Rana's palace. They do not use lavatories.'

'They must use them sometimes,' Ved said surprised.

'No, no. You see, the custom is, when the Rana wants to' — he hesitated and ended daintily'—pass a motion, he will clap his hands, and one of the concubines comes running with a silver pot. Into this the Rana—ah—passes his motion. In the old days they used to do it while receiving guests. It was very'—he searched again for a word and came up with a rather surprising one—'irritating for the guests.'

'It must have been,' I said. 'What happened to the pot?'

'The concubine took it away and it was strewn on the fields as fertilizer. The excrement of a Rana was thought to be the best fertilizer. The peasants vied with one another to get it.'

He laughed and added dryly. 'It was the one useful thing the Ranas gave Nepal.'

Gupta panted up the stairs a few minutes later. He greeted the professor, kissed the children, avoiding nose-drips, and said, 'I have been following you from the pillar to the post. Would you like to look round the valley?'

'How many towns are there in the valley?'

'The valley is only thirty square miles. There are three towns, Kathmandu, Patan, and Bhatgaon. But Nepal is 53,000 square miles, you know, and if you want to see it properly you must go up in the mountains.'

'Let's look at the valley first,' Ved said, 'then the mountains."

'To go to the mountains you need horses. You can visit Thoka, Pokhra, Halembu, villages like that, for two days. But we can visit all the three towns in the valley in one day. By jeep.'

'I think,' the Professor said, 'they should also visit Kirtipur and Bhuttha.'

'Ah, Bhuttha you must see,' Gupta said.

'That is the Buddhist stupa, isn't it?'

'Yes,' said Gupta, 'I have a jeep below. Let us go.'

The state religion of Nepal is Hinduism, but there is also a Buddhist section of the community. In this, however, the two religions have interfused to such a degree that a totally new kind of Buddhism has emerged. It has little to do with pure Buddhism, and not very much, though more, to do with the Lamaism of

Tibet, which again is something distinct from Buddhism proper. The connection between Lamaism and Nepalese Buddhism lies in the fact that the majority of Nepalese lamas, like the majority of Tibetan lamas, belong to the Mahayana sect, in which the clergy are allowed to marry and have personal possessions, as opposed to the Hinayana sect, a rather more Trappist body. Bhuttha is the stronghold of Buddhism in the Kathmandu Valley. There is a great stupa, or Buddhist relic-shrine, in the village, and also a kind of monastery where lamas live, and a colony of Tibetan refugees. The whole community is ruled over by a Mahayana lama whose ancestors came from China through Tibet five hundred years ago and founded the stupa. He is called the China* Lama.

There are conflicting stories about the China Lama. The previous night we had been told that he had three wives and several dozen concubines in his house, that he brewed liquor in the basement, and that he extorted contributions towards the upkeep of the stupa. Gupta, today, said this was not exactly true.

'As to the number of his wives,' he said, 'I do not know. He certainly has many children. As to the concubines, there are many beautiful young girls on the premises, and naturally, people suspect that he has orgies, but I do not think that is so. He is really a very clever fellow, one of the cleverest in Nepal.'

We left Kathmandu by a dirt track climbing across a ridge or backbone of small hills. The sun was burning in the meridian, and the monkeys and buffaloes in the green rice fields by the road were swaying in a dazzle and stupor of heat. We went through a couple of villages, deserted save for the inevitable red peppers spread to dry on dirty clothes. The third village we came to, some five miles outside Kathmandu, we entered through a carved wooden gateway. A circle of mud-brick houses, thatched and patched and dusty, this village, and at the centre the stupa

---

* Pronounced Chee-na.

protruded from stone paving, the shape of a woman's breast, nippled with a staring golden mask of Buddha.

The jeep stopped at the end house and we followed Gupta up some more circuitous wooden stairs. One flight up, we passed through a curtained doorway, and the China Lama, sitting cross-legged on a chair fanning off the flies, canted a round, unevenly shaven melon-head sideways and looked at us through eyes small and dark as melon seeds.

He wore a crimson robe which left one plump, blue-speckled shoulder bare, and he stretched an arm out to shake hands. We sat down on a sofa. The room was furnished like mother's parlour in Tooting, except for strings of rosaries and scarf-offerings hanging on the wall. Through the single window the sun glittered from the blank golden face of the stupa's Buddha-cap.

'So,' he said in English, 'you authors from England are?'

'We have been there,' Ved said.

'Oh!' said the lama, rounding out his mouth and huffing slightly with his cheeks. 'You like?'

'Yes,' I said.

'You no surprise I can talking English? Many people very surprise, they come from whole world me to see, and always I can talking their same language. China Lama is most educated fellow. Twenty-four languages I can speaking.'

He told us what they were.

Gupta said, 'Lama sahib, Mr Moraes has come from seeing the Dalai Lama.'

'Ha! Good you are seeing that boy? He good boy, he Dalai, Rimpoche,* see? I his man.'

'In Kathmandu?'

'In all Nepal. All Nepal is knowing China Lama. Dalai Lama say he want any most little thing in Nepal, then China Lama is getting, see? You Buddhist boys are? Why for no? I Buddhist,

* Beloved: a title given to highly placed lamas.

I very good man, Dalai Lama Buddhist, he same to same God, see?'

I lit a cigarette. The China Lama shook his sharkskin-coloured head at me.

'I no smoking, no drinking, and I sixty-nine, going on seventy. Everybody say China Lama same to same forty-year-old man. See, I Buddhist, I doing what Buddhism say, Buddhism say, no must drink, no must smoke, no must make jig-jig with the ladies. I not doing like that, see? So I looking same to same forty.'

This aboriginal conversation was beginning to pall on all of us. Ved switched to Hindi, which was one of the China Lama's twenty-four languages.

'But that is Hinayana. I thought you were Mahayana.'

The China Lama brushed this aside. He burst into linguistic pyrotechnics and all his twenty-four languages turned the room into a tower of Babel. Most of the languages were incomprehensible Nepalese dialects, but there were snatches of Bengali, I thought I caught a few French phrases, and once he said *Jawohl.* When he had ended, a little breathless, he sat bolt upright and smiled at us.

'See how well China Lama can speaking? Now I show for you our postures of meditation.'

He turned his eyes to heaven and struck a succession of poses, naming each one as he did so. When he had finished, he recited a Buddhist prayer, wagging his finger at us, gravely.

'You want any more? I will do for you.'

'Thank you very much,' I said, 'we mustn't trouble you any further.'

'No trouble. Now I will telling you something how I live.'

He wagged his finger a little more and said, 'At three I waking up. Then half an hour I walking, to take some air. Then I eating some egg, then two hours I meditating.'

He showed us how he meditated. 'Then I praying. With one hand I turning prayer-wheel, so, with one hand I reading prayers. Two hours I praying.'

I tried to work out what time this would make it, but gave up.

'Then I drinking some tea, our Tibeti tea, I seeing my disciples, I eating some vegetable, for rest of day. Sometimes I going Kathmandu. Never I drinking, never smoking, never I eating except some egg and some vegetable, never I making jig-jig with the ladies, three hours I sleeping. You like?'

'Fine,' I said, and Ved said, 'Now we must really go.'

As we were leaving, a thin young man crept in on all fours. He crawled to the China Lama's small, plump feet and kissed them. The lama with one foot waved him aside into the corner.

'My disciple,' he explained unnecessarily. 'He fool.'

As we were leaving, I glanced back and saw through the window of one wing of the China Lama's house a number of exceedingly pretty Tibetan girls. They smiled at us and made 'Come-up-and-see-me' gestures: but we passed on.

I felt depressed, and Ved's lower lip protruded a little sulkily. Gupta alone remained cheerful.

'You have seen one of the great men of Nepal,' he said.

'It would be interesting to meet some Tibetans,' said Ved, ignoring the last remark. 'Do you think that is possible?'

Gupta stopped between two straw mats and asked the woman who sat sentry over the peppers drying on them. She nodded to a house close to the China Lama's.

'She says there is a great lama there who was abbot of a monastery in Tibet. Shall we see?'

'Yes,' said Ved with a determined look, and though I felt the whole expedition had a doomed quality about it, I trailed along.

We climbed more narrow stairs to the small room which the lama occupied. It looked out on to the stupa, it was furnished only with a chest-of-drawers, an iron bedstead, and a mattress on the floor. On this the lama sat. He was a tall, wiry man with a Sioux face, seamed deeply along the cheeks and forehead. His pigtail was wound round his head, forming a sort of bun at the back. He had wispy Tibetan moustaches, and two gentle slits for eyes. On the floor by the mattress lolled a young Nepalese, and standing on the far side of the room a Tibetan woman, obviously the lama's wife.

He was sipping butter-tea, when we arrived, out of an earthenware bowl. He looked up as we entered; his eyes rested on us, mild and inquiring. Gupta explained our visit to the young Nepalese, who translated into Tibetan. The lama smiled and thrust his tongue out at us in greeting. Then with a gentle float of his hand he invited us to sit on the bedstead.

The room was cool; a little breeze sifted through it. The walls had a few pictures of Tibet, cut out of newspapers, glued to them. On the floor by the bed was a small charcoal stove topped by a gently fuming iron tea-kettle. The lama asked if we would like some tea.

We said yes, and his wife fetched it to us, with worn careful hands, in the earthenware bowls, and with it a biscuit-tin full of small sugar-cakes. The language made conversation difficult: it had to come from the lama to the young Nepalese, from him to Gupta, and from Gupta to us. But all the while the lama smiled and turned toward us, touching us gently and alternately with his eyes.

'He is the Alakirti Lama from the Ando Monastery in Tibet. He came in 1956 even before the flight of the Dalai Lama.'

'Why did he come then?'

The lama gave a rueful little smile, turning his long hands outward to explain. His voice was deep and soft, but quick; he talked in little eddies; he clearly wanted us to understand his precise meaning, and because that was impossible the smile came often, rueful yet friendly and searching.

'He says his mind is very restless; he has no peace here; he regrets that he came. He came because the Chinese were taking the lamas of his monastery for forced labour, and confiscating the goods of the monastery; it was impossible to meditate or pray. But he wishes now that he had stayed: he says it is better for a man to die in his own country than to pray to the Buddha in someone else's.'

Gupta told the Nepalese that I had seen the Dalai Lama in Delhi. It was translated, and the lama made a swift little smiling gesture of benediction.

'Rimpoche says that it gladdens his heart to know that people from across the black waters are friendly to the Dalai Lama, for the Dalai Lama is the whole of Tibet, and without him there could be no Tibetan people. He asks if you are interested in Buddhism.'

'Very much so. He is Mahayana, isn't he? Ask him the difference between Mahayana and Hinayana.'

The lama looked thoughtful; then he explained, again with that queer simplicity that groped towards a perfect statement, tapping his pen case on his knee as he made a point.

'Rimpoche says the Hinayana do not mix with the world. They know no women, who are half the world to any man; they pray and fast in solitude. The Mahayana go forth into the world, they know women, and speak to other men. Thus by Hinayana a man attains Nirvana through himself; in Mahayana he attains it partly through others. Yet both are equal, for both are part of the Twofold Way.'

I had a sudden memory of a book about levitating lamas which I had once read. I asked about levitation.

'Some lamas say they can levitate, but Rimpoche has not seen this. He says for himself, man has enough grief on the ground, why should he wish to take it into the air?'

Ved asked how old he was. The lama looked puzzled for a second. Then he gave a gentle smile of apology and, lifting his heavy wooden rosary from the mattress beside him, told his years on the beads.

'Forty-seven.'

'How long has he been the abbot of Ando Monastery?'

'Too long,' said the lama with his smile.

'What is Ando like?'

The lama answered slowly, clicking his beads in his fingers. He bowed his head, and did not lift it till the translation had reached us.

'He says, once it was a small green field on the southern side of heaven.'

Gupta paused to laugh appreciatively at this, then went on:

'They had their yaks, and their land, they worked on the land, they prayed and honoured the Buddha, till the Chinese came. He says that the last time he saw Ando the Chinese were leading the young monks, bound, to Lhasa, and the western courtyard was in flames.'

The lama rose and went to the chest-of-drawers. He returned with a photograph. 'That is Ando.'

The picture was small and blurred, and brought no image to one's mind. When I handed it back the lama looked at it for a minute as if he did not really see it. Then he presented it to me.

'He wishes you to have it so that you may remember him when you are across the black waters.'

And round Ved's neck with the gesture of benediction, the lama hung a Tibetan scarf.

We rose to go. 'Tell him that we hope that soon, when the Dalai Lama is back in Lhasa and the Chinese have been driven from Tibet, he may return to Ando and live as he did before.'

The lama said something gently, laid a hand on my shoulder and looked at me for a long time. Then he did the same to Ved.

'He says that will not happen in his lifetime, but he thanks you for your good wishes. It has gladdened his eyes to see you. Nobody has come to him before from across the black waters. He will keep your faces in his heart. Go with God.'

The two great temples of Kathmandu are Pashupatinath and Swayambhunath. On the way back into town we stopped at

Pashupatinath. It is a place of pilgrimage for Hindus from all over Nepal and India.

The gateway was of carved wood, gaudily painted: gods with dry-rot on their foreheads surveyed us as we advanced towards the steps on bare and tentative feet. A riot of children appeared crying for alms. 'Give to one and you get a hundred.' There really were hundreds; those who were able-bodied mobbed us; the weaker children fell back, wailing softly, and returned to scrimmaging in the sacred rubbish heaps with dogs and langur monkeys.

Inside, down a flight of stone steps, the main temple stood in a sunken courtyard, surrounded by smaller buildings. There were sadhus everywhere, entirely naked, squatting under trees, with dusty beards and small, drugged eyes. One leant on a parapet, his face a mass of overgrown beard and hair; his flesh was ridged and yellow, like tree-bark. 'He is a very holy fellow,' Gupta said. 'He has been standing like that for the last twelve years.'

A noise of drumming and chanting rose from the temple. A smell of dead flowers and incense filled the air. It was all frenzy: an immobile frenzy drove the sadhus. Before the doorway of the temple stood a brazen bull, fifty feet long. The facade was of stone, carved with little wicked gods. We climbed the steps and stood before the sanctuary.

In the sanctuary, a small square cell, the air was thick with incense. Flowers lay at the feet of the god. I could only see the feet from where I stood: cubelike, unthinking stone toes, fallen arches. Three priests moved among all this; old wood-coloured men, warped in the middle, tortoise-necks writhing, naked under saffron robes that left the jellied flesh of the right shoulder bare, their faces smeared with red and yellow paint, incessantly wailing, mumbling, feeding the censer so that smoke poured blindingly up. One came to the window, mumbling toothlessly and extending a finger of his right hand. I felt a wet dab on my forehead, and then his left hand came up and lassooed my neck with a garland of dead flowers. For a minute I had a trapped feeling; then he let go. I did not wait for Ved and Gupta but hurried back to the jeep, surrounded by weeping, naked children; I gave them all the change I had, but more and more came, and more, and I was besieged in the jeep, rubbing again and again at the place of my forehead where the tika of wet sandalwood paste had been dabbed, and distributing English pennies in desperation, when the others arrived.

When we got back to Kathmandu we went straight to the bar of the only European hotel, off the Jyuddha, and ordered large brandies. The place was still under construction and the bar was full of carpenters hammering and sawing. There was only one other customer. Ved and I took the first drink in silence, while Gupta went on about plans for the next day. I rubbed the place on my forehead and did not say anything much.

'Anyway,' said Ved, 'it was an interesting day.'

'Yes,' I said. 'I wonder what the China Lama is doing now.'

The other customer at the bar gave a little jump of surprise. I glanced at him. He had taken off the crimson robe and had on an American bush shirt and palm-beach trousers, but it was still the China Lama. He was drinking a double whisky.

It was worth everything. I leant back in my chair and burst into helpless giggles.

The China Lama pretended not to hear.

A Village with No Walls

A flute playing in the garden dragged us out of bed next morning. Pannalal was clattering in the bathroom with buckets of hot water for our baths. It was very blue crisp weather outside, so I tried to whistle 'Greensleeves' till Ved, whose colic was unabated, implored me not to.

I went down instead, after my bath, and stood benevolently in the sunshine till Gupta arrived in a jeep.

'What do you wish to do today?' he asked.

I looked up to where the Himalayas stood, green shadows against the sky. 'Go to the mountains,' I said.

'Why not? While it is good weather you should go. Otherwise in rain it will be difficult. But you will have to spend the night there.'

So I went and told Ved, who continued to mourn over his stomach. We packed a toothbrush and a razor, and we left the palace at nine.

There were no clouds in the sky. The driver sang happily, and Gupta beamed at us. 'We will get horses at the foot of the mountains. We will visit Thoka, perhaps. Typical mountain village of Nepal. On the way we will see Patan and Bhatgaon.'

Patan is a little way up the valley from Kathmandu. It lies amid paddy fields, not a town really, a patch of town, starting suddenly and tailing away into huts to the east. There was a market on, when we arrived: wooden stalls had been put up, cluttered with fruit and vegetables: people bargained shrilly, but nothing ever seemed to be bought. We pulled into the centre of Patan, around a small temple-filled courtyard, which included a squat and celebrated Hindu shrine carved out of a single rock. The gateway to the courtyard was lined with the shoes of devotees. I had decided that I did not like temples, and the shoes were off-putting; it was almost as if they might get bored and come flip-flopping out while their owners were still prostrate before the god. One of the priests emerged, coughing and blowing his nose with his fingers. The smears of ochre on his face were roughed with sweat.

Gupta, who is a Hindu, advanced and made the namaskar. The priest replied. He was like a Catholic priest in some backward Italian town, planted like a fat persimmon in the sun, strong in parochialism, with bored eyes. His first words were even more reminiscent.

'The people do not make offerings at the temple as they used to. They are swollen up with selfishness and wickedness. I will teach them, I will teach the godless ones: no more blessings shall I give till there are offerings at the shrine again.'

He said this not so much in conversation as in proclamation, and the bystanders stirred uneasily and flickered an eye at each other. I cut in: 'How long have you been at this temple?'

'Twenty years. These rapers of their sisters have felt my wrath before now. If they are not respectful to the servant of the gods, he will blast their crops on the day of the harvest!'

'What is the history of this temple?' Ved queried. The priest looked at him with a severely practical glint in his eyes.

'Give me money and I will tell you.'

'Go to hell,' said Ved in English, and turned away.

But the priest raised one arm in the air, flapping and croaking.

'I know what it is that you say! Evil one! Have you no respect for the servant of the gods?'

The bystanders began to mutter ominously, obviously seeing an opportunity to reinstate themselves in the priest's favour without spending more than a little energy.

'We have annoyed him,' Gupta said. 'I think we should go.'

So we left Patan under something of a cloud.

Bhatgaon was much the same, only wilder, more straggling, with the same mud houses, and we hesitated in the main square, and finally Gupta said, 'Shall we continue?' and we said 'Yes, rather,' and so went on.

The mountains were closer, they rose towards us, always larger, and the track climbed through foothills, and eventually we had to get out and push, there was so much mud. Then we lumbered like a military tank to a village in the shadow of the Himalayas, and there stopped. Gupta climbed out.

'We will get horses here.'

The villagers gathered round us. They talked all together, quickly, and their hands slewed up and down. Gupta ignored them.

'They are not the owners of the horses. Keep close to me and do not enter into negotiations with elsewise persons.'

So Ved and I got out, and stood silent in a storm of voices, till Gupta, who had nipped up the street, returned.

'The horses are ready. Let us go.'

There was a short pause, while we instructed the jeep to come back the next day. Then, trailed by our adherents, we moved farther up the street to the headman's house, before which three sidling ponies stood, saddled, but rolling crimson nostrils, and gently and angrily flattening their ears.

In the midst of their pirouettes, we seized them, I feeling piratical, and came aboard. The saddles were wooden and horned, and hurt as soon as one sat on them. A trail of villagers clung to us, shouting, as we wheeled the ponies around and trotted out of the village.

It was midday.

For the only time in my life, I felt slightly anxious about Ved. As I bounced on the wooden saddle, I decided I must keep an eye on him. I was much aggrieved when he came cantering back down the bridle-path.

'Are you okay, Dommie? Do you want a hand?'

'No,' I said sourly, and followed the other two thereafter.

The road was steep, rock-strewn, and occasionally flooded. Progress was slow. Every now and then the ponies had to tiptoe along the edge of a precipice. At first it was all right: the precipice was low to the ground, and a fall would have meant a cut elbow, perhaps, and reminded one happily of one's childhood. Later it grew higher; a fall would have meant a broken neck. My pony insisted on the edge, and I kicked it despairingly. Occasionally, squinting down, I would see clods disintegrate from its hoof, and its previous foothold rain down crumbwise into the valley beneath.

All round the mountains got bigger, hairier, more menacing, and the valley dwindled to small Chinese roofs and rivers like saliva-threads from the sudden lips of the hills. I held the reins, pressed my knees tight into the pony's sparse ribs, and hoped. Finally we emerged from the edge into an area of trotted-up slopes, the trees steaming mist on either side. I had to lean forward on the pony to keep in sight of the others, and also, with the mist steaming in through my shirt, it became exceedingly cold.

'Are you all right?' Gupta shouted back through the mist, and I replied haughtily, 'Excellent.'

Then more climbing. The pony stuttered his feet every so often, and yawed his head back, and squiggled his behind, and riding became agony. The mist had fortunately blotted out any prospects of a fall, and my entire consciousness was concentrated on avoiding the next bump. Eventually we climbed to a village, where people came out and stared amazedly.

'Is this Thoka?'

'A few miles yet,' Gupta shouted back. 'Do you wish to dismount?'

'Yes,' I said, and slipped off into a dung-smeared street.

A girl came to my side, like Florence Nightingale, and said, 'Do you want a drink?'

'Yes,' I said again, and she brought me some Nepalese beer in a copper bowl.

I drank it and felt slightly better.

'Come on, Dommie,' said Ved enthusiastically, still from the saddle. 'We must go.'

We did, then, scrambling up a steep track dissolving now in the faint mountain rain, always higher; the wooden saddle unbearable each time the pony trotted: but luckily that wasn't often.

Finally, in the mist, the ponies clinging with slithery hooves to the edge, lights glimmered in the stew ahead, and Gupta called 'Thoka' back to Ved, and Ved called it back to me. So I stuck my heels into the pony's side again, and managed to arrive, at a species of canter, in a village of nervous mud huts sticking to the mountain. People came out to stare. We dismounted and looked around.

There were about twenty huts in the village, mud and thatch; a single narrow street; goats; a pig. The headman came out and showed us to his hut. We had been riding for five hours. Women brought us tea and a kind of popcorn. The doorway of the hut was filled with the rolling pony-eyes of villagers, darting away when we returned their look.

The hut itself was a low two-roomed building, with blackened beams across the ceiling, from which brass and copper utensils and ladles dangled. The only furnishing was a rope bed, on which we sat, and in the corner a broken-legged chair. The headman squatted on the floor in front of us. He was a wiry middle-aged man with quick eyes and bristly cheeks, over which he kept rubbing his hand.

'Where have you come from?' he asked, and when we told him nodded, impressed. 'You come from the capital. I welcome you. My name is Thapa.'

We exchanged namaskars and he said, 'How long will you honour us with your presence?'

'May we stay for the night?' Gupta asked, and Thapa spread his hands wide.

'It will be a privilege for us. We will give you a feast.'

And he clapped his hands and summoned his wife, and said to us, 'Do you drink spirits?'

'Some of us more than others,' said Ved, and the headman turned to his wife and said, 'Bring the drink of three waters.'

The wife returned in a few minutes with four copper bowls and a copper jug. She filled the bowls with a transparent liquid that had a curious smell of dry grass. Then she brought a copper dish with bits of pickled lime in it, and went away.

'Drink,' Thapa said; so I lifted the bowl and drank deeply.

It was as if the top of my head had been blown off. I closed my eyes and blew my nose. After some critical moments I felt a little better. I even laughed a little at Ved, who had just taken his first swallow.

'You don't like it?' asked Thapa, disappointed.

'It's remarkable,' I said. 'What is it?'

'We brew a liquor of one, two, and three waters. The difference is in the length of time it ferments. This is of three waters, the best and the oldest.'

'It's very good,' I said, and drank the rest. It got better, like most things, the more you drank. Also if you kept a bit of pickled lime in your mouth when you drank, as Thapa did, it went quite smoothly. One bowl of it, however, was enough. I staggered slightly when I rose.

The mist had lifted, and outside a damp world waited. The air was cold and good. We walked through the village. People came out of their huts to watch. Some of the young men joined us. They were small and sturdy, their cheekbones higher and their skins fairer than those of the people in Kathmandu, and were very friendly.

'It is time for the singing,' one of them said. 'Come and listen.'

'A concert?' I asked.

'No, no,' said the young man, laughing. 'You will see.'

A pale distinctive twilight; we walked to the edge of the village, where it abutted on the forest path. Scarlet hibiscus made wreaths among the trees. Thapa pointed.

'It is the guras,' he said, 'the flower of the mountains.'

The path came down from the mountain, lined on either side by enormous shadowy oaks. It ran parallel with the village for fifty yards then curled down the mountain again. The young men—there were about a dozen by now—lined up by the curve, some sitting on boulders, some standing. Gupta explained to me.

'The girls from the next village have gone up the mountain to cut firewood. Soon they will pass by, and the young men will sing.'

And while we waited in a twilight full of expectant whispers, other voices came from farther up the path, the bird-clear voices of girls, and seven or eight came into sight, each carrying a sort of wicker pannier full of firewood, walking with a swinging mountain gait towards us. The flowers of the hibiscus were twined in their black hair.

One of the young men stepped forward into the path, spreading his arms like wings to block their passage; a little self-consciously, swaggering a little, thrusting his chest out, he began to sing. It was a high wavering tune, with dying falls, as if a flute should have a voice and sing words. As he sang, he made cajoling gestures with his hand, looking uneasily every now and then at the other young men, to see if he was doing well. But the others looked embarrassed, and turned their heads away for the most part: a few laughed in the twilight, slapping their thighs. The girls had gathered into a little knot vividly miming first surprise, then anger, then indifference; but all of them cocked their dark eyes at the young men, and occasionally they giggled. At last, when the first singer had done, another took his place, and later another. The young voices piloted the high tune into the twilight gathering now to night, till it was lost; and at last the young men stood forlornly in the silence, looking at the girls.

Then one of the girls stepped forward. She gestured the young men out of her way, she stamped her foot, she mimed anger. Then she sang. Her voice was a soaring treble that broke on the high notes, but as she sang some of the other girls joined in, till it sounded like a little choir. The young men laughed again, freshly, and slapped their thighs: then the girls laughed too and moved forward, and the young men gave way. And the girls went on down the long path, still singing; and even when they had turned the bend and were out of sight the clear pure singing came back through the cold air. The singers stood staring after them long after they had disappeared, with their faces pleased and longing at the same time, like puppies after their feed. Mist came again, and we walked back into the village.

The young men cheered up on the way, laughing loudly and slapping each other's backs. I walked with Ved.

'What do you think of that?'

'It was very strange, Dommie. They were like little Nepalese angels.'

I walked ahead and caught up with the first singer.

'That song you were singing, it's very beautiful. What is it?'

'You like it?' he said, pleased and flushed, and the others laughed, slapping his back harder. 'It is an old tune of our people.'

'What are the words?'

'Oh, those we make up as we sing.'

'You improvise them?' I asked, genuinely surprised.

'Oh, yes. Each of us sings what he wants to say.'

'Can you remember what you said?' I asked.

'I can try.'

So I asked him back to the headman's hut. The other young men came too. We were all given copper bowls full of the liquor of three waters, and slices of pickled lime. Ved and Gupta talked to Thapa and the young men in one corner, all rapidly getting very drunk, and the first singer and I sat in another. Charcoal braziers were brought in by the women, for outside night had fallen in a final mist.

I got an old envelope and jotted down a translation of what had been sung to the girls:

'Since your childhood you have picked the red flowers from the
hibiscus tree.
Sixteen summers I have watched those flowers fall,
*But as yet I have not climbed to the summit of Dhaulagiri,**
As yet I have not understood the hearts of the people of Nepal.
Queen of the mountains, hibiscus-fountain, goddess of Dhaulagiri,
Come quickly, be gentle: the old men say time flies:
Come quickly to the forest, where your father will not see us.
Show me the hibiscus flower between your thighs.'

'What did the girls answer?' I asked the young man.

'I do not recall: they improvise their words too.'

'But did they say yes or no?'

'They said, "Not today,"' replied the young man, and laughed immoderately. 'That is what they always say.'

'But do you do this every day? Is it a custom?'

'No, not a custom,' said the young man. 'We do it because we like to do it. Who does not like to sing?'

Later, when we were all very drunk, the women brought in spiced buffalo meat and flat wheat pancakes, boiled eggs, and curds. Thapa tasted the food first, then the rest of us served ourselves. We each had a dish of beaten copper to eat off, and one of the women produced a teaspoon, but nobody used it. After supper bowls of warm water were fetched, for us to wash our hands in. Then we sat on the floor and smoked.

---

* A Himalayan peak.

'How long have you been headman?' I asked Thapa.

'Fifteen years now, ever since my father died. I am fifty years old.'

'You were a headman under the Ranas, then?'

'Yes,' Thapa said.

'Did you have much trouble under them? Taxation, things like that?'

'We were too far up in the mountains for them to bother us,' Thapa said. 'Sometimes, yes, sometimes they came, they took a pretty girl now and then. But even then, unless she was married, nobody objected. It was good for the girl; the Ranas fed and clothed her better than we could do in the village: what more could she desire?'

'Happiness?'

'My friend, you are sentimental. Happiness is to be fed well and clothed well. Even Devkota says that in his poetry.'

'Who is Devkota?'

'He is our great poet,' Thapa said with pride. 'He is the poet of the people of Nepal.'

'He is dying,' Gupta put in. 'He has cancer of the intestines and he is dying in Kathmandu.'

'Dying? Hai mai! What misfortune have the gods brought to Nepal?' There were tears in Thapa's eyes. 'It is hard that a poet should have to die.' He clutched his drinking-bowl, lifted it, and said, 'Let us drink to Devkota.'

So we all joined in the toast. Afterwards I said, 'Do you get books of poetry here?'

'Not books, my friend. I cannot read. But the poems of Devkota are repeated among us Nepalese. If my brother were here, he would recite some, but he has gone to Bhatgaon. Devkota was a sensible man, you see, for a poet. We can understand what he means, and it is always good sense.'

After a while Ved asked, 'What is life like in this village?'

'It is our life. It is as it has always been. The families who live in this village have known one another for two hundred years.'

'You live off the land?'

'Yes,' Thapa said. 'We grow the things we eat.'

'What happens if there is a bad season?'

'If one family's crops fail, the other families help it. After all, if the entire harvest fails, we would all starve together; so if one field does not bear, we all eat together. There are no walls in our village.'

It was past midnight. Thapa said, 'I have prepared a hut for you. Do you wish for women? My youngest daughter is a virgin.'

We said no. Thapa laughed.

'Too tired? That's right, it's no good when you're tired. But if there is anything else you desire, tell us and we will bring it.'

The hut had three rope beds in it, each with a straw quilt. It was cold; we were all tired and full of alcohol; we slept. I awoke sharply in the small hours to hear a deep creaky roaring outside. It died away into a muttered snarl, and then began again.

Ved was awake too. 'What's that?'

'Tiger, I think,' I said.

We listened, but there was no further sound. So we fell asleep again. Thapa's wife awoke us, bringing buckwheat cakes and raw onions for our breakfast. We washed at the well. Most of the villagers were standing round, including some of the young men from yesterday.

'Was that a tiger in the night? We heard something—'

'Yes, a tiger,' one of the young men said. 'He came quite close. The fires he did not like, therefore he roared. But he went away.'

'Do you have many round here?' I asked.

'No; it is too high for tigers. A few come, not many.'

He added, 'It is clear weather.'

'Yes.'

'If you climb a little higher,' the young man said, 'you will see Dhaulagiri and Everest. I'll come with you.'

We left Gupta in the village talking to Thapa, and climbed the slope. We took the path down which the girls had come the previous day. The guras bled through green leaves everywhere. As we climbed, the forest grew thicker, and the path little more than a furrow through the undergrowth. Brilliantly coloured birds flew away at our approach. There was no sign of human habitation anywhere, except here and there a felled tree. Presently we turned off the path, struggled through the forest for a hundred yards, and came abruptly into the open. We stood on the rocky lip of a precipice, moustached all over with smooth green turf. Purple and yellow poppies grew in the grass.

Our guide advanced to the edge of the precipice, and waved his hand outward.

'That way is Tibet, and there are the mother-mountains.'

I looked out from the precipice. In the brilliant sword-bright air one was able to see for miles, like an eagle. Ranges of small mountains, rocky or forested, stretched away before me; and at the very farthest point to which the eye could reach, beyond the hacked and rivered flesh of the smaller ranges, projected a line of snow mountains, like a row of teeth. 'Everest,' the young man said, 'Everest is one of those. Also Jalpaiguri and Dhaulagiri.' He paused, smiling back at us, lowering his pointing arm. 'Is that not beautiful?'

'Have you ever been that far?'

'Only with my eyes,' said the young man, smiling. 'Come, we must go back.' On the way down he plucked some guras flowers. 'If you have girls whom you love in Kathmandu, give it to them, that they may put it in their hair.'

'It's a very kind thought,' Ved said, 'but they are a long way farther than that.'

'Never mind. Keep it for them. The guras is red for many days.'

When we left the village Thapa and some of the young men walked with us a little way. None of us said very much, but smoked and spoke of the weather. The neck of my pony was hung with red flowers. Finally, where the track tilted steeply back toward the valley, Thapa stopped.

'We will go now,' he said, and smiled. 'Come back soon.' 'Come back soon,' the young men said, and we rode on towards Kathmandu, and I was sorry, because I did not think I would ever be able to come back.

Dying Poet

'Do not be too unmindful of the dead.
Keep Kashi* burning.'
—L.P. Devkota

Next morning we were visited by Dr Suman, the Indian cultural attaché. He is one of the leading Hindi poets: a large man with a heavy laughing face and thick black wings of hair stroked back from a centre parting. He burst into our quarters unannounced, followed indignantly by Pannalal, and flung his arms round me, crying, 'At last two poets meet!'

I agreed, after he had introduced himself, which he did not do for some while. I was feeling grumpy and a little saddle-sore.

'How long you are here for?' Suman asked.

Ved had to be in Calcutta the next day, in order to fly back to Harvard. 'Only another day.'

'A pity, a pity. But this evening,' he said, 'lots of poets can meet. I will ask all the Nepalese writers to come to my place, and we can hear their poems. You like drinking, eh?'

'Yes,' I said.

'Good! Which poet does not like? But now,' he added, 'I must take you to the ambassador; he wishes to meet you.'

We dressed, rather painfully, and went down to Suman's car.

---

* Benares: city of burning ghats.

It was a large Buick and he drove rapturously, frequently taking both hands off the wheel just to show us that he could.

'You should really have met Devkota. He is the greatest of the Nepalese writers. But his poor soul is flying away on the dark wings of cancer.'

He thumped me on the knee and shouted, 'Good phrase, eh?' The ambassador lives above the town, in a house with broad verandahs, surrounded by rose-gardens. He gave us tea on one of the verandahs; a host of dachshunds came and arranged themselves round our feet; it was like tea at Julian's house in Gloucestershire, even to the extent that the ambassador did a little painting and sculpting. Suman took me round the house and showed me the end products framed tastefully on every wall, or standing on occasional tables. There was one rather striking head of Han Suyin, enigmatic curly smile and all.

When we came back to the verandah, the ambassador was talking to Ved about Dickens. Eventually he turned to me with a charming and tactful smile, and said, 'I understand Dr Suman is arranging a meeting for you this evening with the Nepalese writers. It is a pity you could not meet Devkota.'

'We've heard a great deal about him,' Ved said. 'Is it possible to get his work in English?'

'He has himself translated some few things,' Suman said.

'A really great man,' the ambassador confided gently. 'It is a real tragedy that he is dying. The Nepalese queen mother offered to pay for his treatment in Russia a month ago, but by then it was already too late; now the doctors have given him two days.'

'Where is he now?'

'In hospital,' said the ambassador. 'But the whole history of his treatment in the last week is very peculiar. You know that the Bagmati, which flows through the valley, is a holy river? Well, the custom is, when a man is dying, his relatives carry him to the banks of the Bagmati and leave him there. The Pashupatinath temple faces the river on one side, and most people in Kathmandu are taken there. Last week his relatives carried Devkota there and left him for two days, but he did not die. So they had to take him back to hospital. Now they definitely think he is on the point of death, and apparently they're planning to take him back again.'

'He is a great man,' Suman said suddenly. 'He is a great poet. It is difficult with such a limited language as Nepalese to be a great poet, but Devkota has done it. Not only that, but by his work he has altered the entire course of the language.'

'And he is a very intelligent fellow,' said the ambassador with pitying eyes. 'And when he speaks, it is a kind of poetry: he thinks in poetry. I went to see him in hospital and he was not at all self-pitying, indeed he was sardonic. He said that while he was waiting to die by the river, with his relatives already singing his death-hymn, he determined that he would not die that day and be hurried off to the burning-ghat, simply because they all seemed to be anxious that that should happen.'

Ved and I sat silent. I said, 'I would like to pay him my respects.'

'He must be dead by now,' the ambassador murmured sadly, and looked deep into his rose-garden.

Later the professor called on us at the palace, bringing half a dozen students with him, three boys and three girls. They sat like mice while he held forth for a short while, nervously, on education. Then he waved at the students.

'Talk to these gentlemen,' he commanded.

The students looked at each other; then one of the girls said; 'Is England nice?'

I said yes, very. There was another silence, then another girl turned to Ved: 'Is America nice?'

'They know all about you,' said the professor with a contented chuckle.

'How are the cosmetics in England?' asked the first girl. 'Do they use lipstick there?'

One of the boys interrupted:

'What are the politics in England?'

'The government is Conservative. That is to say, a right-wing party. The opposition is Labour and Liberal. They are '—I hesitated for a description—' much the same as the Conservatives, really.'

'No Communists?'

'Not very many.'

'Then I shall not go there,' one of the boys said firmly. 'I am a Communist.'

The other boys nodded. The girls mocked them.

'Oh, you think of nothing but Communism.'

'And you think of nothing but cosmetics.'

'What are your politics?' a boy asked. We both said we were liberals.

'That means nothing,' said our questioner (I privately agreed). 'You must be Communists.'

'How would you apply your political views to Nepal?' asked Ved.

'We must have Communism.'

'Yes, but in what way?'

'We must,' said the boy firmly.

'Do many students belong to the party here?'

'Very many male students, yes. The girls are frivolous and do not care for issues of the day.'

'What would you say are the major issues of the day?'

'Communism.'

This went on for some time, then the professor nodded at them. 'You must go.' When the door had closed behind them, he turned to us. 'Those are my most intelligent pupils.'

'They all take English, do they?'

'Yes; but as you see, they are more interested in politics than anything else. They once supported Koirala's Socialist programme, but there has been a lot of CP activity in Nepal, and K.I. Singh has turned into the hero of the young people. Practically all the intelligent students are Communists.'

He added, 'They know nothing about it. But partly because they think Koirala is selling out to India, and partly because China is so close, they want Communism.'

When he left he said wistfully, 'I wish you had explained a little about the democratic system of government to them.'

'It would have been difficult,' Ved said.

'I suppose so,' said the professor.

In the evening the poet son appeared and said rather frostily, 'I am to take you to Dr Suman's party.'

'Ah,' said Ved, 'are you coming? How nice!'

His poor little olive branch withered at the poet's eye. 'It is after all a meeting of Nepalese writers,' the poet said. 'They cannot hold it without me.'

'And shall you read a few of your things?

'No. I only read to select audiences.'

We drove in silence to Suman's house.

Suman lived in a villa on the outskirts of the town. He came out to the trellised porch to greet us, and slapped us all on the back.

'I was unable to find any pretty ladies for you to talk to; they are all men,' he said, and led Ved by one hand and me by another into a large sitting room, with tapestries on the walls, where several grave Nepalese were sitting.

One, gaunt and pale, with a beret of starched linen, was introduced as Balkrishna Sama, leader of the old movement. Another, thickset and slant-eyed, was introduced as Vijaya Malla, leader of the new movement. They sat at opposite ends of the room, regarding each other without favour. The remnant were disciples of one or the other.

'Aren't there any of Devkota's disciples?' I asked Suman in an undertone.

'Oh, these are all Devkota's disciples,' said Suman airily. 'Nepalese poetry has only been going on for about fifty years, you know. Sama is the Chaucer of Nepal and Malla the Eliot, but

Devkota is the whole anthology from Chaucer to Eliot, so far as Nepali literature is concerned.'

And he pounded on the table.

'Drink, drink!' he shouted to his servant. 'O *Saki*,* let us look upon the wine!'

Gin and beer were produced, and platters of Nepalese delicacies: baked lentils, boiled potatoes covered with curry powder, tamarind kernels. 'Eat, drink, and be merry,' said Suman, 'for tomorrow we die. Let us read our poems,' he added. 'Sama sahib, you begin.'

After Sama had modestly declined, gradually begun to unbend, and finally put on his spectacles to look up his manuscripts, and we had all sat back to listen, the poet son said sepulchrally from the sofa into which he had sunk, 'This is an evening dull with poetry.'

Sama looked annoyed, Malla laughed, Suman wrinkled his whole face up in a wonderfully expressive grimace of disgust. But then the reading progressed. Each of the dozen or so poets read two poems each, and then translated, and one, Ghimiri, sang his poems. The Nepalese language, though it has its roots in Hindi, seems a more difficult language to handle: it has shorter words, and, I believe, fewer rhymes. The poems read out did not fall with any particular pressure upon the ear, and from the translations, their content was not particularly remarkable either. The older generation seemed mostly faux-Shelleys, fainting when they touched the night-dark tresses of their beloved. The younger ones indulged in surrealist juxtapositions: Malla, as he read, kept looking at Sama with a little crooked smile, to see if he was shocked. In both cases it seemed that the poets had taken their influences from English via Hindi writers. But the subject matter of both old and new movements was curiously similar: unrequited love, landscape-admiration, and little requests for salvation, though the younger poets occasionally threw in some social comment as

* Cup-bearer.

well. Thus all of them seemed to have a definite public in mind: a public which demanded a certain subject matter, and a certain already defined approach to those subjects. Every now and then, in the midst of the poem, a poet would raise a finger for closer attention and slowly syllable out some image of which he was really proud. All the others would smack their knees at this, with deep belly-grunts of 'Wah, wah,' or 'Shabash.'* Once Suman jumped up and rushed over to one of them and flung his arms round the poet, sobbing deeply and saying, 'Brother! Sensitive soul!' and it took some time to get the reading going again.

When Suman himself read, which he did last of all, his glass of whisky uplifted like a chalice towards which his luminous eyes rolled frequently, his poems were on unrequited love as well. Here again the Shelley influence was perceptible, but this time at one remove, whereas in the Nepalese poets it had been at two and clumsier. I tried to think precisely what it was that I did not like in this sort of poetry, and decided that, in the less advanced of the Indian languages (this excepts only Bengali, which is far ahead of the others) there has always been a restricted and highly conventionalized imagery. When a poet writes in the impersonal way in which most Indian poetry is written, refers, that is, less to himself than to a recognized background, he uses these stylized images as his basis, like a builder with bricks ready to hand. This is the way in which poets like Ghalib write, and it is successful. When the writer cobbles the old images together and adopts, in the poem, the stance of some chosen Western poet, the images lose their quality of ornament, and the stance its quality of power, because the two are fighting against each other.

But Suman loved his own poetry despite the faults he saw in it, which is one mark of a poet, and when he had finished, the tears were streaming down his cheeks. He seized my hand, asking in a choked voice, 'Good? Good?' There was obviously no room

* Well done.

for criticism here, it was not like someone throwing the latest manuscript over to one in the pub, so I said, 'Wonderful.' He beamed and cried, blowing his nose, 'Now the piece of resistance: you must also read.'

I recited two poems, a little nervously. I recite rather slowly, and they clearly thought that an ovation was required at each pause, and with Suman as cheerleader shouted, 'Wah, wah,' and banged their glasses on the tables between every line. This was very cheering. I laboured to the end and then had a long drink. Sama said, 'Devkota would have been glad to see you.'

'We fly away tomorrow,' I said.

'What time?' Suman said.

'Twelve-thirty,' Ved said, and Suman nodded.

'Is Devkota still alive?' he said.

'I saw him today, in the hospital,' Sama said. 'He is nearly dead, he can hardly speak. Tomorrow they move him to Pashupatinath to die.'

'I will arrange,' said Suman. 'I will arrange. Devkota will be happy. Any poet would wish for another poet to stand and wave at his train, when he says goodbye.'

I woke very early and went to the window as the sun struck free from the Himalayas: a welter of burning clouds: and then suddenly the same sun, like a new-minted coin floating over mountain and valley and river, a blue sky, and the Chinese roofs of the town showing up in the bright cold light.

It was our last morning in Nepal.

Peculiar, to leave a place. 'When I return,' I thought, 'if I return, I shall be older, stiffer, less drunk, more settled: I shall stay in a hotel and have breakfast in bed. For by the time I return there will be a Hilton Hotel, and there will be a motor-road to Thoka, and we shall drive there to take photographs of Everest. And the same for Ved.'

But meanwhile Pannalal was sneezing his way out of sleep, and

Ved was climbing through the mosquito-curtains and looking for his dressing gown. 'Hallo, Vedkins,' I said.

'Hallo, Dommie. Where the hell did I put my dressing gown?'

'Foot of your bed. I say, do you realize we're leaving today?'

'Yes. We shall have to send some telegrams.'

'Let's not,' I said. 'Far nicer to arrive in Calcutta with nothing fixed.'

'You old romantic,' Ved said, laughing.

'That's one of the things about leaving a place, one always has to send these damned telegrams. If we don't, we'll be able to breathe our way out of Kathmandu, not just leave, destination Calcutta.'

'Okay,' said Ved tractably. 'But I must send one to my father.'

'Come to think of it,' I said, 'I must, too.'

Pannalal fetched the hot water. We shaved and washed, and in the middle of it Gupta arrived.

'Suman says you want to pay your respects to Devkota. I will take you.'

'Is he in hospital still?'

'They have carried him to Pashupatinath today. He may die at any moment.'

'Oh, I say,' I protested, a little absurdly, 'one doesn't want to disturb him at this time.'

'No, that is all right. He will be glad to see anybody, especially two writers. He is alone, you see.'

We dressed, and went down to the jeep-taxi. 'Drive,' said Gupta to the taxi-man, 'to the ghats of the dead.'

It was a long drive, through the valley lying green and brilliant all round, before we bumped down a slope into a dusty village. The usual children surrounded us, asking for alms. Gupta waved them away like a cloud of gnats.

'The jeep can go no farther. The temple premises are down there, and the Bagmati beyond.'

We walked down from the village to where a wooden gateway let us through to an unpaved courtyard. Women were drying red peppers in the sun, and the overflow of children and dogs from the village harried our ankles. Little heaps of dung, from different sources, lay about.

'This is the temple.'

At the other end of the courtyard was another wooden gateway, and through this we saw the river, the Bagmati, a brown languid grease scumbling over stones between two wide banks. There was an extraordinary smell hanging over it, an unmoving, pervasive smell: a smell partly of burning, partly of excrement, and partly of death.

We walked down a flagstoned pathway, the river at our right. On our left a line of one-storeyed buildings, with stone floors and pillars, and wooden roofs, ran down to the long stairway leading into the temple. Two wooden rafts floated on the scummy surface of the Bagmati. Gupta pointed to these.

'There must be two people near to death. They will be cremated on those.'

A few steps farther there was a concrete projection into the river. 'That is where the king is cremated, and the Ranas.'

And then, pointing to one of the buildings on our left: 'The house of the dying. There we will find Devkota.'

This building consisted of a stone-pillared verandah, on which wooden trestles were laid, about ten feet apart. On most of these trestles lay undistinguishable figures, swaddled in sheets, most of them attended by one or two bored relatives, some unattended. The relatives hummed, in appropriately sepulchral voices, the final hymns, but there was an undersong, a deep tortuous humming, and as we came nearer we saw what hummed it: the verandah was black with flies; great clusters buzzed along the floor, and around the heads of the dying. A priest lolled on the steps, fanning himself to keep the flies off. He glanced up as we came.

'Where is Devkota?'

'The poet? I think he is dead.' He rose, yawning, and glanced leisurely along the line of trestles. 'No, not yet. There he is.'

He pointed, and we edged past the foot of deathbed after deathbed, till Gupta stopped, bowing deeply, and making the namaskar.

On the trestle before us a man lay on his left side with a dirty white sheet drawn up over him, so that only the top of his head showed. A woman with her sari over her face, in token of mourning, squatted by his side, fanning the flies away. Gupta said softly, 'Devkota sahib. Devkota sahib,' and the woman drew the sheet away from Devkota's face.

We moved to the side of his bed, and the woman signalled that we should sit down. One hand never ceased moving the fan over Devkota, so that the flies could not settle. We squatted on the floor.

The face that we saw was a mask, with thick dark hair drooping dryly above. Beneath the hair was a fine forehead, with large eyes that opened a little to look at us. Below the eyes the face had fallen in: the cheeks like craters, the lips sunken and wrinkled like a very old man's. But from under the dirty sheet two long hands projected from stalklike, sand-coloured arms, crept slowly together, and made the namaskar.

Then again the beautiful eyes closed, and he lay still on his side, his hands fallen. He breathed in deep painful sighs, and between each breath gave a faint moan. We sat in silence. Phlegmatically, the woman moved her fan.

After a long pause, Gupta introduced us. The eyes fluttered open. They were brown eyes, inanimate as lakes, so far had they gone into death. But when something struck them they reflected it: in flashes and for seconds. They were naked eyes.

One thin hand groped painfully over the mattress towards us.

I grasped the hand in both mine and squeezed it. It was very cold and dry. There was a long pause. Then the mouth unpuckered from its creases of pain. Very slowly, groping and whistling, it said: 'Cosmic conflagration….'

The woman, with the same complete resignation as had marked all her other movements, produced a chipped green thermos flask from the head of the bed. She opened it and took a lump of ice out. This she fitted between the poet's lips.

He sucked it for a while, still looking at us. Then he whispered again, 'I am in a cosmic conflagration...'

None of us said anything. The mask twitched in a summoning of strength.

'I am burning. This is like hellfire. Nothing...man has not invented a torture that can equal cancer.'

We were still silent. He whispered at me, 'I have read your work.... I know your friend's name also.... It is a miracle to find you here as I am dying.'

'We wanted very much to see you, sir,' I said.

'Cancer...it burns me, I am dying. If I was alive I would show you my poems. Have you seen my poems? Tell Sama,' he whispered to Gupta, 'to give him my poems.'

Then to me: 'Some of my poems I tried.... I tried to translate. Translation is a very difficult work...but I did my best....'

His eyes closed, he had gone away from us, and again came that faint regular moaning. The woman put another bit of ice into his mouth. After a while he looked at us again.

'I have so few words left to say.... I want each one to mean something...but now there is nothing I can say. They gave me blood transfusions: they said they would keep me alive a few days longer. But I grew tired of drinking human blood. So I have come here to die...

'My poems were too materialistic...they were too much of the world...but I will not renounce them. I am here in the temple of Pashupati, I am dying. But somewhere there is one inch of me left...one atom of me left, that will not allow me to let go. I pray that I may let go...if the god Pashupati were to come, I would beg him to crack my skull....'

He looked at us again, striving to say something with his eyes, but could not, and wearily they fluttered shut, and wearily opened again.

'You see before you the carcass...of a man who once weighed 175 pounds. Now it weighs fifty-two...it is a carcass...there is one inch of Devkota left...one atom...that too will die. What is the use of lingering here, in this misery? Pray for me...pray that soon I may die....

'They called me a Communist, because I went to Russia.... I was only a poet...pray for me...pray for Devkota, that he may die....

'Even if I go into hellfire, it would be better than this...pray that I may go quickly...for me... I am the most unfortunate of the writers of Nepal....'

And suddenly the mask tried to cry. The sunken lips twitched, but could not sob: they were too far divorced from human function: only tears slipped down from his eyes, to make lakes in the deep crater of his cheek. I clasped his hand in my hands, and at last he looked at me again. 'Recite some of your poems...let me taste a little peace.'

I came closer to him, so that he could hear properly, and began to recite.

I had just begun, when from one of the other beds came a wail of women, high and monotonous; the priest came rushing from the steps, officiously; somebody had died.

Devkota paid no attention; he fixed his eyes on mine and whispered, 'Recite.'

I went on. When I had finished, Devkota sighed. Behind me the relatives were carrying the dead man out to the burning-ghat. Devkota whispered one of the lines.

'"Earlier in Time I prayed to be forgiven..."'

And then, strengthening, 'Recite another.'

And when I had finished: 'You are a much more natural poet than I was.... I was always more mechanical...too professional... there was so little time.' And for the only time he tried to smile. 'You will forgive me for that?'

I squeezed his hand again, and he whispered, 'Recite some more.'

'I'll recite somebody else's,' I said, and thought of Edna St Vincent Millay's 'For Any Dying Poet':

> *Time cannot pluck the bird's wing from the bird.*
> *Bird and wing together*
> *Go down, one feather.*
> *No thing that ever flew,*
> *Not the lark, not you,*
> *Can die as others do.*

Devkota said, 'Yes, that is beautiful.... The image in the first three lines is bad...but I understand...it is true, perhaps....'

Gupta touched my arm and said, 'Your plane. You have only just time.'

He said to Devkota, 'They must go. Today they are flying to Calcutta.'

Devkota whispered, 'Will you not stay...two writers...will you not stay till I die?'

And I said, helplessly, 'I suppose we must go.'

Again the mask trembled, trying to weep. Then the lips quivered together. 'Give me your blessing on my road,' Devkota said. 'You both have mine on yours.... Go then.'

Ved and I both bent and kissed his forehead. It was like his hand, already cold. With a great effort he lifted his hand in the sign of benediction.

'Pray for me.'

So we walked away from that place. We stumbled through the dusty courtyard back to the jeep. My eyes did not seem to focus on anything properly. From the Basumati a plume of evil-smelling smoke rose, gently tickling the nostril, from the pyre of the man who had died.

Spider City

We packed quickly, thanked the general, who wished us better health, tipped Pannalal, who did not thank us, and drove to the airport to find the plane was late. So we fed off our fingernails till it came, and then rose over the Himalayas, rose away from the Chinese roofs and the dying poet and Thapa and the palace, and three hours later came bumpily down at Calcutta.

Rain poured from the sky: it was like landing under a waterfall. The great airport was full of people going somewhere. We stood in a floodlit lobby, feeling small and unimportant, while the rain hammered on the roof and the bus stood snoring placidly outside. When at last we left, all the roads were flooded.

The bus ferried us into the city, through flickering miles of tenements, past rows of lighted shops crowded with Bengalis prodding their umbrellas at the lightning, and decanted us at the terminal. We stood there, small and unimportant again, and discussed policy.

Eventually we got a taxi and drove round to several hotels. They were all booked up, and it was still raining. We wound up at a large hotel in Chowringhee, the main street. Crowds insected through Chowringhee, traffic lights flared green and red, pachydermatously the buses and cars shuffled through, umbrellas gleamed, rain fell, and Ved said bitterly, 'Here we are.'

We went into the hotel, up a stairway carpeted in red, with

flunkeys saluting us everywhere. This was clearly going to be expensive.

It turned out to be the most expensive hotel in Calcutta. We took the cheapest sort of rooms, not air conditioned, that is, and went up to them. Ved collapsed on his bed and groaned: 'What about money?'

'We are running short,' I said.

'Short! We shall have to write articles for the newspapers. Rush jobs. It's going to be just like London, in a month when one's broke.'

'Oh, for Christ's sake!' I said. 'Forget it and let's have a drink.' 'What do you feel like?'

'Champagne,' I said.

So Ved rang for a bottle of champagne.

When it came we suddenly broke out into laughter.

'It's no use, Dominie,' Ved said. 'We do have expensive tastes.'

After we had drunk the champagne we felt better. Ved said, 'What shall we do now?'

'There is a very good poet somewhere here,' I said, 'called Buddhadeva Bose. Let's get hold of him.'

We looked round. 'Where's the telephone?'

There was none. Ved rang for the bearer.

He came, a plump and satisfied man, rubbing his hands together, with a noise like the scraping together of two biscuits.

'Where's the telephone?'

'There is no telephone, sir.'

'Why not?'

'What is the use of a telephone, sir? Who uses telephones?'

It is the only time I have ever seen Ved really angry. He stamped both his feet. I had only seen this done once before and I stared in fascination. Then he smacked his hand with his fist.

'What do you mean, who uses telephones? What sort of talk is that? Go away. Go away quickly.'

The bearer looked suddenly discomposed. He squinted nervously at Ved for a minute, then hastened out. Then came shoutings in the corridor outside, and finally the bearer reappeared. He carried a tray. On it was a telephone. The flex trailed gracefully behind.

'My God!' I said, and began to laugh.

The bearer was hurt. 'I did my best, sir. Do you not like this telephone? It is a nice telephone.'

'Yes, yes. Very nice. Thank you.' I tipped him and he resumed his former poise. I looked up Buddhadeva Bose in the directory.

The pattern of the evening was already forming. Buddhadeva Bose was out.

'Now what?' Ved said.

'Let's go and have a look at the town.'

'I'm told,' Ved said meditatively, 'that it's full of vice.'

'Good!' I said.

Because I suddenly felt very tired, ill, foolish: Devkota was with me, he would not let me go; and I was so lonely for you, to tell you, to help myself by telling you, that it paralysed me: Devkota's face floated above an image of swans and the Thames and a sunny day. Perhaps it was only the champagne. As a child I used to go away by myself, when I felt like that; since growing up, I take myself into crowds instead.

The bearer was still hovering round. 'Where's the nearest bar?'

He named it.

'Is it lively?'

'I do not know, sir. I do not drink. But there was a murder there last month.'

'Then,' Ved said, 'it must be lively.'

'Only uneducated fellows go there, sir,' said the bearer warningly. 'My friend has never been educated,' Ved said.

We got a taxi and went to the bar. The city seemed vast: it was still raining, and neon winked sardonically through the rain. It was strange after Nepal.

The driver turned back to us. He was a Sikh.

'You looking for——?'

'No, we don't want food, we want a drink.'

'Not food, sahib,——. You not know——?'

Ved was quicker than I was.

'No, no. Just a simple drink.'

'Why you going that bar if you no want——? Very cheap there, very quick, they having beds upstairs. Otherwise you coming with me, I getting you fine girl, whole night spending, she know everything.' He lapsed into Punjabi.

'What's he saying?'

'I think it's better for you not to know, Dommie. It might corrupt you.'

We reached the bar, in a street of neon. As we got out of the taxi a thin man in pyjamas came up.

'You want——?'

'No,' I said. I was orientated by now.

'Very fine girls. Anything you want. English, French, German, Anglo-Indian, Indian, anything. I know one Spanish also.'

'No,' Ved said, and we pushed him out of the way.

'—— not wanting, —— not getting,' said the taxi driver from behind us.

'You philosopher, you,' I said.

We had to climb a floodlit flight of stairs to get to the bar. It was all one packed room, with a square of dance floor, and it was full of sailors. They were mostly English, but one heard Norwegian and French when the music stopped. This was not often. There were tables, all taken up, and a counter from which a huge forlorn cuckolded phonograph projected its horn, and the dance music brayed, and the couples dancing seemed to be anticipating the beds upstairs. In one corner of the room sat a row of decrepit Chinese and Anglo-Indian taxi-girls.

We found two seats at a table: an English sailor and two Chinese taxi-girls were in the other three.

'What colour is your brassiere?' the sailor kept saying.

The girls held the front of their dresses open, and the sailor peered in, looking a little bewildered.

'Pink,' he said finally, with an air of triumph, 'and *black.*'

'Do you like black brassieres?' he asked me.

I said, 'Very much.'

'Why not let's all go to bed together? The five of us? I know a way for five.'

'Some other time,' Ved said.

'Well, have a drink with me anyway,' said the sailor.

So we all had a drink. The taxi-girls said nothing, and the sailor tended to wander a bit. Presently another sailor came up. He had a broken bottle in his hand.

'Do you want to fight?' he asked.

'Get the hell out of here!' the first sailor said. 'Can't you see that these are my friends?'

'Well, that's all right, but what about a fight? Just a little one.'

'No. These are fine chaps. They like black brassieres.'

'Oh,' said the sailor with the bottle, impressed. He wandered off.

'Low class of clientele they get here,' said our sailor.

We ordered another round. One of the girls said, 'Do you want to dance?'

'I can't dance,' said Ved, lying, and I, being truthful.

The sailor put his head on the table and went to sleep. Presently he opened his mouth and was sick. 'I think we should go,' I told Ved. 'Come upstairs with us,' said the taxi-girls. 'Next time,' I said.

As we went out, two Anglo-Indian teddy boys came up. They had sideboards and leather jackets. One of them had a flick-knife in his hand.

'Do you want to give us your money, chum?'

'No,' I said.

'Oh well,' said the teddy boys, disappointed, 'if you don't, you don't.' They went away.

Outside, a man came up to us. 'You want first-class?'

'No.'

'Very fine. Very clean girls, English, French, German, Nepalese, African....'

'Oh, off,' said Ved despairingly.

More bars, more sailors, more whores, more pimps, and finally Ved said, 'It would be interesting to talk to some tarts.'

'What about, for Chrissake?'

'Oh, their life, their work, that sort of thing.'

'What are you going to ask them about their work?'

'Don't be coarse, Dommie. Prostitutes are interesting people. I once read a book....'

'If you want to talk to a whore, I must say it seems pretty simple here.'

We went outside. A lean Cassius-faced man came up to us.

'You want ——? I got fine selection, English, French, German, Chinese, Indian, very clean girls, all virgins.'

'How much?' Ved said.

'You want quick one or whole night?'

'Half an hour,' Ved said.

'Ten rupees for the girl and two for me.'

'Oh, all right,' I said.

We all got into a taxi. The pimp sat in front. The taxi driver, again a Sikh, turned to us.

'You not trusting this man, sahib. I knowing him well, he uneducated fellow[7], taking you uneducated girls. I knowing some fine girls, English, French, German....'

'Don't listen him,' said the pimp. 'He bad fellow, I not uneducated man, I going to college, failing BA.'

I could only remember an appropriate aphorism of the painter Francis Bacon: 'Put not thy trust in ponces.'

We drove into a narrow street, the houses leaning over us, narrow jigsaw-puzzle houses: no neon here, a dark world.

Presently the pimp waggled his hand and the taxi pulled up. We sat in the dark, the pimp had disappeared, and the taxi driver began a jeremiad:

'It is a pity that educated people like you falling in clutch of such fellows. Terrible disease you will get.'

'Where's he gone?'

'He gone getting girlies.'

Then the pimp came back.

'Lovely ladies coming,' he said, 'you wait, I not uneducated fellow, I bringing you real Jean Harlow girls.'

And two girls came sidling along the pavement, in short tinsel frocks, and stopped by the taxi. One of them thrust her head in the window. Her cheeks were ash-coloured with the wrong shade of powder.

'Don't you fancy us?'

'No,' I said, frankly.

We drove on. 'Uske umer bahuth uper the,' the driver said. 'They were aged girls, nearly thirty. You see how this fellow is cheating you.'

We circled into another street of dark houses. 'Nepalese girls here,' said the pimp. 'Young girls.'

He slipped something into the driver's hand.

'Sahib,' said the driver, 'I can tell you, this good house, nice girls here. This fellow fine fellow, not showing you wrong.'

The pimp returned. Behind him, walking on quick furtive mouse-toes, came two very pretty Nepalese girls. They were made up very heavily, and they stopped by the taxi.

'Do you want them in the taxi or do you want to come up?' asked the pimp.

'In the taxi,' Ved said.

So they climbed in. They smelt of some very strong Indian scent. The one next to me put her arm round me.

'No, no,' said Ved at the other end of the seat, 'you don't understand. We only want to *talk* to you.'

'We want to *talk* to you,' I told my girl, but she clearly did not follow.

'No, not that,' Ved said desperately. 'Talk. *Bathchit.* Understand? *Je veux parler.* What is talk in Nepalese, Dommie?'

'You pleased, eh?' the pimp said from the front seat. 'They very passionful.'

'Yes,' I said. 'Go back to where they came from.'

'You want go upstairs?'

'No. I want them to go upstairs.'

'You not like?'

'We tired, we sick, we going home,' I said. 'We pay.'

'You want us to undress?' my girl asked a little angrily.

'Why don't you ask them a few questions about their work?' I said bitterly to Ved.

We got back to the hotel reeking of Nepalese scent, and I said, 'I think we probably need another drink.'

We drank some brandy. Then I went to bed. I was awoken an hour later by Ved.

'For Chrissake,' I said, 'it's two o'clock!'

'I know. But we weren't very brave. Let's go out and talk to some prostitutes.'

'It's two o'clock.'

'I know. I know. But you wouldn't want all the taxi drivers to think us cowards, would you? We aren't cowards, are we?'

'Yes. Go to sleep.'

'We shall always be thought of as cowards, Dominie. We must talk to some prostitutes.'

I was just drunk enough to think this a reasonable argument. 'Oh,' I said, 'all right, all right.' And I dressed.

We went out and got a taxi. 'You want——?'

'Yes, yes, yes, yes,' I said.

'What kind of girl?'

'Any kind girl,' I said.

'No, Dommie. They must be indigenous.'

'Indian girl having,' said the driver, 'Anglo-Indian girl having. Indijuns girl not having.'

'Any kind of girl.'

So more narrow streets, and another house. The driver went up. He returned with two girls in saris.

'Lovely girls. Same to same film star.'

We got out. The girls disappeared into the house. 'Stay here for twenty minutes,' I said to the driver, 'otherwise I will eat your life.'

We climbed a flight of narrow stairs. They smelt like a urinal in Paris. The girls were waiting at the top.

They were both about sixteen, with mascaraed eyes, cheeks smudged with rouge, and the lips crimson with betel. They led us into a long room with benches in it, and we sat down.

The girls sat next to us. I suggested that Ved should begin to talk.

But before he could do so, a flock of girls came through the opposite door and sat on the benches as well. They were mostly Bengali girls, but there were a couple of Chinese, and a negress. All of them were in their twenties: they wore tinsel saris, or short cocktail frocks: all had carnivorous mouths of betel-lipstick. They sat down and giggled.

'You must choose,' said the first girls.

'We only want to talk,' said Ved piteously.

'The best kind of talk is done in the bedroom, light of my eyes,' cried the African girl passionately, and tried to unzip my trousers.

I leapt up in the posture of a Botticelli virgin and said, 'We must go.'

But three men stood at the door. They were small hairy men, with absurd pouting betel-reddened lips, and absently they were paring their nails with large knives. They looked at me and smiled, still absently, but pared their nails with great flourishes thereafter.

The girls fluttered away, leaving an aura of chypre. We were alone in the long room with the scent and the nail-parers. We walked towards them, with the sensation of coming down a long narrowing gangway. When we reached them I said, 'Get out of the way.'

The first man smiled pleasantly and turned the knife in his hands so that it pointed at my stomach. He said nothing.

I grasped Ved by the arm and plunged towards the doorway. We thumped softly, once, against the men; they disintegrated suddenly and we stumbled down the odorous stairs to the taxi.

Wind inflated my shirt, which had a neat knife-cut through one side. 'Back to the hotel.' The taxi driver greeted us with a fraternal smile.

'You having good——?'

'Wonderful,' I said.

'Yes, this good house.'

'We didn't have time to talk,' said Ved, disappointed.

The spider city winked its neon eyes.

It was four in the morning when we returned to the hotel. I slept till four that evening. Then I woke, shaved, drank a raw egg, and telephoned Buddhadeva Bose. I had never met him, but knew him by name as one of the leading Bengali poets. He is one of the four stars that flamed in the wake of Tagore. The others are Amiya Chakravarty, now in America, Bishnu Dey, and Sudhindranath Datta. All these poets have translated their own work into English, and some of it has appeared in the West.

Bose was in this time: he asked us to dine with him. I asked him to drink with us before that: eventually he said he would meet us at the hotel. We were drinking in the bar downstairs when he arrived: a very small man, with a keen and extremely beautiful face, a wide sensitive mouth, and thinking eyes. With him was his son-in-law, Jyoti, and a tall American, the poet Galway Kinnell.

Kinnell was on a Fulbright scholarship; he was on his way to Teheran, to teach there. He said little at first meeting, and Bose, too, was mostly silent: he left his son-in-law to do the talking. But once we had settled in the garden with our drinks, he began to talk, and at once I felt that peculiar and extreme gentleness which most poets carry with them like a cloak. 'You will be long in Calcutta?'

'I don't know,' I said. 'Ved has to leave tomorrow, but I want to go up to NEFA if I can.'

'Stay a long while,' Bose urged with a quick smile. 'It's rare that other poets visit Calcutta, and there is so much here to write about.'

'Are there many young writers?'

'All the young Bengalis are writers, but there aren't many good ones. A few. I'll arrange for you to meet them, if you would like that.'

'Where do they publish?'

'Well, I run a poetry magazine. *Kobita.* It has been going for twenty-five years. I was a boy when I started it, but we have grown up together. Shall we go now? The women will be waiting for us.'

'There's some Indian whisky,' Jyoti said. 'My brother-in-law said that he would get some ice and soda. He made me swear that Mr Kinnell and you were both poets. He never does anything for people who aren't.' So we got a taxi and went out into the warm rain-smelling night.

'They are bloodsuckers at your hotel,' Bose said. 'You ought to come and stay with me. I live in the Indian part of Calcutta: we are going there now. You ought to see that: it is better than this in every way.' We drove quite a long way, fetching up in a wide teeming street where radios wailed from the eating-shops, and cows mooned along the pavement. Bose lived in a flat above the street. We climbed to it and went inside. Bose's young son came out to greet us, his hands folded in welcome. His two daughters and wife emerged quietly from the kitchen, were introduced, and returned.

The room we sat in was cool and quiet. We could hear the trees sifting the wind outside. There were books everywhere, paintings, a desk: the sofa and chairs were covered with rough hand-woven cloths, beautiful and cheap. Everything in the room had a look of use about it; even the paintings were paintings that had obviously been used by quiet eyes.

Jyoti brought in some Solan whisky, cracked ice, and glasses; we drank. The soft bird-murmurs of the women stirring in the kitchen came to us occasionally, and a faint smell of cooking. Bose began to talk about Tagore.

'Nobody has ever realized, in the West, the extent of Tagore's influence on Bengali literature. He is more than our only great poet. He was our first great novelist: he wrote about eighty novels. He was our first great playwright. He wrote criticism that shaped the thinking of all the younger writers. He painted pictures to illustrate his poems, and he composed the music for his songs. He was a colossus: I think even in world literature there has never been anyone quite like him.'

'Did you know him?' Galway Kinnell asked.

'I knew him when I was a young man. It was the greatest honour possible to a young poet to be taken to see Tagore. We used to cut our hair, put on fresh clothes, chew cloves to make our breath sweet, and then not have the courage to say anything. That didn't matter. He talked all the time. He was very conscious himself that he was doing one an honour; he liked to patronize young men a little. He looked magnificent too, with that white beard and the high forehead. It was terrifying. Of course, his voice was rather squeaky, that was the only thing that made one feel he was human at all.

'He was a great man. He invented new metres, he refurnished the language and he was Bengali literature while he lived. There was Tagore: then there was nothing. For a young poet, it was difficult to grow in his shadow…'

The women came in, bringing dinner: Bengali food, soya beans and wheat-cakes and the famous hilsa fish, prickly as the coelacanth. Afterwards there was fruit, which the women quickly and neatly skinned for us. Then Bose brought out a dusty bottle of Benedictine. We sat drinking it slowly while Bose read out some of Tagore's poems. He read in an intent whispering voice, with a long pause between each line. The poems had a pure, lighted sound: strange to me, who have read Tagore only in English, and not liked it. Bose said at the end: 'You see what a great craftsman he was? He could say anything, but he always said it beautifully, musically. And it is true what Yeats said, "We must labour to be beautiful."'

He closed the book; we rose to go. Bose remained in his chair, smiling at us. 'You must come again, soon. Telephone me, Dom. We will come here and read some poems and create some peace.'

Ved was leaving next morning. I saw him to the terminal. He would be in London in three days, and standing outside the airlines bus, I told him to give my love to various people. I felt awkward, involved in the mechanism of a goodbye.

'It was quite a good time,' Ved said finally. 'Goodbye, Dommie. See you in New York some time.'

'Goodbye,' I said. 'Be good.'

I stood waving rather pointlessly on the pavement for a long time after the bus had pulled away.

Sargasso Time

'A tract of ocean covered with floating weeds.'

After Ved had gone, I started spending most of my day writing. It was so hot that I did this in a cold bath, the typewriter balanced on the soap-rack, the shutters pressed back like eyelids over the windows to keep the glare out, so that the room was in semi-darkness. It was very peaceful like that, but got a little lonely. I was glad when Jyoti called me up one afternoon and asked if I wanted to meet Jamini Roy.

Jamini Roy is perhaps the best known of Indian painters: the maestro figure. He has held this position since the 1930s. I remember, as a child, having a painting of his in my nursery, 'The Last Supper': small, flat bright-coloured saints with fish-shaped eyes, rigid in identical poses on each side of a small, flat bright-coloured Jesus. When Jyoti arrived with Galway Kinnell to pick me up, I recalled this.

'He's painted hundreds of Last Suppers,' Jyoti said with a smile.

'Really?'

'Yes; he has a few apprentices, you see: when he wants to get some paintings ready quickly, he draws the outlines and the apprentices paint them in. Then he adds a few finishing touches and signs it, and there you are, another Jamini Roy. The Last Supper is one of his favourite subjects for rush jobs.'

Jyoti was slender and bespectacled, with curly hair and a curious air of being simultaneously thoughtful and excited over everything. He made a strong contrast with Galway, big and powerful with a square jaw, features that seemed hewed from some pale grainy wood, and unchanging blue eyes. For a moment I looked at them both as though they were a painting, listened as though they were disembodied voices: Jyoti giving the world away in a word, Galway, in a soft Princeton drawl, giving away nothing.

We drove through the glaring afternoon. Jamini Roy lives in a white house away from the centre of Calcutta: a disciple in white robes opened the door for us; he showed us inside, to a long white-walled room. One felt drenched in coolness, though there was no fan. Perhaps this was due to the spaciousness of the room: it was totally unfurnished, save for benches along the wall, on which new-looking paintings were propped. The two adjoining rooms were similar. We walked from room to room looking at the paintings. They were all painted in the same manner of a highly stylized primitive: often there were seven or eight in a row, identical except for the colours: Last Suppers, Annunciations, and the three kings going to find Jesus, three bearded triangular-eyed figures poling a skiff over a curly two-dimensional ochre sea. It was a purely decorative kind of art. There was no real reason why any of the pictures should exist; yet they existed, and propped up like that against the white walls, they seemed to come out of a legend, and to form a world.

When we had looked at all the paintings we paused and looked at each other. We were alone: the disciple who had let us in had gone away. The rooms smelt faintly of paint and cedar wood. 'Jamini Roy will come soon,' Jyoti said. 'He generally has a nap in the afternoons.' We stared at the paintings; they smiled at us.

After a while there was a soft murmur of voices and the disciple appeared at the doorway, looked in to see if we were there, then stepped aside. Jamini Roy came in, an old man, in spotless white robes, folding his hands in welcome and smiling. He had white hair and a high forehead: a face in which, as in the faces of many old writers and painters, the lines were those of a sage or of a saint. Jyoti hastily stooped down to touch his feet in reverence.

Jamini Roy lifted him with one hand, and signalled to the disciple with the other. The disciple went out and returned with some wooden stools, and we sat down in a little semicircle. Jyoti explained who we were, and added that Ved would have accompanied us save that he had to leave.

Jamini Roy listened, then turning to me said that he had heard of Ved, and was he blind? Yes, I said. The painter gave his curiously sweet, illuminated smile, and began to speak. He had a soft husky voice, and spoke in a mixture of English and sign language.

'Painters are same as blind people. They also must see with nose and ears and fingers. But not quite same: they have their eyes. But sometimes they too must shut their eyes to see clearly. I would have liked to see your friend.'

'You paint a great deal?' Galway asked.

'It is my life. I paint always. When I am not painting with my hand I am painting inside my head. All those colours and shapes are always there: I am the one who must stretch my hand out and break them from the air, like fruit from a tree.'

The disciple came with cups of cool water. As we sipped it Jyoti and Jamini Roy spoke together in Bengali. Every now and then the painter gave his sweet smile, so that I thought at first Jyoti was being witty; then I realized that he was not, that Jamini Roy smiled whenever he felt happy.

'Are you a Christian?' I asked. 'Your subjects quite often seem to be taken from the Bible.'

'The Christian books are full of colours to paint with, if you look in them. I look in them. But no, I am not a Christian: I am a painter.'

And he began to ask me about England, about my plans for the future, and my methods of writing poetry. He seemed genuinely interested in them all. Meanwhile, the disciple was explaining some of the paintings to Galway, who was nodding rather vaguely. Jamini Roy smiled again.

'Do you like any of these paintings? Would you like one?'

Galway and I protested, but Jamini Roy shook his head.

'Choose one, if you like any of them.'

So at last Galway chose a blue cow feeding a calf, in a border of lotuses, and I chose one of the three kings in the boat. The disciple fetched them from where they stood, and then handed Jamini Roy a brush. He signed each one and smiled.

'I am glad you like my paintings.'

'Sir,' Galway said, clearly emboldened by his smile, 'I'm told your disciples complete some of your pictures.'

'Yes,' the painter said. 'They do as the disciples of the Renaissance painters did. That is not important. It is not the single painting that matters: to paint is my life, and one episode on the way is nothing in relation to the whole.'

He looked keenly at Galway. 'Is that not true? Do not poets feel the same?'

And, turning back to me, 'You must paint as you breathe.'

After a while we got up to leave the shady white-painted room, with the paintings standing quietly around the walk. The painter stood quietly in the midst of them, with folded hands, saying goodbye with a smile.

Later that day Galway dropped in at the hotel for a drink. The heat of the day had gone and the fan no longer washed one in warm air, but in cool. But it had been hot enough before to make us both tired, and even cluttering the drinks with crushed ice did not quite take the dust out of our throats.

I told him about the visit to the brothel, and he laughed.

'I thought it was much more glamorous than that in India,' he said. 'I thought it was all Oriental and silky.'

'Not this place,' I said. 'But in Benares it's certainly more Oriental.' I told him about the nautch-girls.

He looked interested. 'That sounds more like it. I'd like to see that.'

'I don't know if they have that sort of thing here,' I said. 'I could ask Jyoti.'

Jyoti, on the telephone, sounded surprised. 'You want to visit a brothel? My dear fellow I really wouldn't advise it. It's very dangerous.'

'Not professionally,' I said. 'But you know these nautch-girls, don't you? Galway wants to see that.'

Jyoti laughed and said, 'There's a special Calcutta type. Go to Bow Bazaar, you will find them there. But be careful what you do. And if Galway is going, on no account settle for the first price they offer. If they see an American they will try and fleece you.'

Galway and I sat on for a while, drinking. I didn't really want to go and watch dancing-girls, but two days of more or less immobility in the hotel demanded breaking. Finally I said, 'Well, we'd better go.'

Our taxi driver was again a Sikh. I told him to go to Bow Bazaar. He squinted appraisingly at us.

'No,' I said, 'we want to see a dance.'

He grunted in his beard.

We arrived in a crowded and noisy street, and pushed through to a narrow tenement. Noises of radio music came from here. People were asleep on every landing, swaddled like corpses in sheets. Preceded by the taxi driver, who kicked the sleepers to one side whenever they got in his way, we climbed three winding flights of stairs spattered with betel-spittings, and finally knocked at a little door. A man opened it and stared at us. He was a south Indian, wearing the sacred thread and a cotton sarong. The taxi driver jerked his head at us and said, 'They want to see your woman dance.'

'That's all?' asked the man. When I nodded, he glanced at us and said, 'A hundred rupees for half an hour.'

'No,' I said. 'Do you think we're Americans?'

'Your friend is.'

'Are you mad?' I said. 'He is a Hindu from Kashmir.'

He stared for a long while at Galway, and finally nodded. 'All right. Fifteen rupees for half an hour.'

We went in. It was one small room, with a glass-fronted cupboard in one corner, filled with Hindu religious pictures, pink plastic dolls, and cheap English crockery. On the wall above the cupboard was a tinted photograph of a slim dark young woman, heavily made up. The original, dressed in a white sari, was squatting on a cloth-covered mattress on the floor. She was not as young as she had been when the photograph was taken, and her make-up was even heavier: her dark face was ash-coloured with too much powder, purple at the cheeks with too much rouge. Her eyes were more tired than the eyes of the photograph. Also when she got up one could see through the thin stuff of the blouse the dark eyes of her breasts and the curled mouth of her navel, like a second, slightly obscene face wobbling beneath the one on top.

'You want Indian dance or English dance?' the man asked.

'Indian dance,' Galway said.

The woman gestured us to sit on the mattress, while she stood in the middle of the floor, in front of the cupboard, tightening the waist-knot of her sari and shaking her head as if to clear it. The man took a gramophone from beside the cupboard, put a record on, and wound it up. The wail of an Indian film song broke into the room. The woman, however, was tying on heavy anklet-bells, with slow, methodical, tired movements. When she had finished she began to dance. She stamped and shuffled her feet slowly, making the anklet-bells chink, swayed her arms, and rolled her eyes at us with bored seductiveness. When the record stopped she paused, wiping her face with the corner of her sari. The man put a different record on, and she danced with precisely the same movements. In fact they never varied, whatever the music, except that towards the end she ceased to dance at all, trying tiredly to give the illusion that she was doing so by occasionally moving one foot, or fluttering one hand in the air. After half an hour the man stopped the gramophone in the middle of a record and came over to us. We paid him and he said: 'Do you not wish to sleep with her?'

'No,' I said. 'My friend wanted to see a dance, that's all.'

'But, sir, you will enjoy it, she is very good.' His face worked pleadingly. 'I can recommend her, she is my wife.' And as we turned away he said, 'How shall we keep our children? I will give you a reduced price, sir.'

The woman stood with her head bent and her face to the wall. We thanked her for dancing, ignoring the man pleading at our elbows. She came slowly round to face us.

'It is true. How else shall we keep our children? Now that I am getting old, nobody comes to my bed.'

Shamefacedly we pressed a little more money into her hands and fled downstairs. When we got back into the taxi the driver said: 'Good, eh?'

Galway said awkwardly, as though thinking out his reasons as he spoke: 'I didn't like that at all.'

After that evening Galway and I often drank together. We drank usually in the hotel, but sometimes went exploring round the bars where Ved and I had been the first evening. Here, amongst the usual assembly of prostitutes, pimps, and sailors, shouting above the band, or whispering under, we talked about poets we both knew, or about London, or New York. One recalled the oddest things: I remembered a toy shop in a Knightsbridge arcade where I used to go when very unhappy, during my first days in London, in order to buy small delicate glass toys which I later smashed, one by one, in the fireplace of my flat, with a malediction against anything beautiful. Also an evening on the hillside above Agamemnon's tomb in Mycenae, when I pressed my ear to the grass and thought that I heard the old king humming to himself in the beehive cavern beneath. There was a moon above the hill, and I had a bottle of ouzo.

Calcutta seemed conducive to this: in the sweats of daytime and the nostalgia of the night, one fed on memories, drying them up quickly by sucking at them too hard. Also, of course, I was worried, because I didn't know where I was going to go next. All my life since I was fifteen I have travelled light, always thrown things away because I wasn't sure where I would be next day, and cherished a romantic ideal of myself as a wanderer. This ideal became a little ridiculous when one was stuck in a large expensive hotel with the minimum of necessities in one's suitcase, and a typewriter that had jammed through being dropped into a cold bath. The people with whom I had been going to stay in Assam were not available: I bit my nails and wondered.

From all this I was saved by a good angel in a brown suit. He came bouncing into my room early one morning, while I was swearing at the typewriter.

'Hah! You are having trouble with your typewriter? Let me see.' He seized the typewriter and shook it. Then he did something to the reels. Then he said, 'It is done. Nothing like a little mechanical ingenuity, hah?'

'Is it all right, do you think?'

'Certainly, certainly. But we have not been introduced, hah?' He shook my hand. 'I am Ajit K. Das, of the United Press of America. Here is my card. I am also a professor of economics in Calcutta University, and finally, I work for your father's newspaper. It was he who asked me to look you up.'

'I think Marilyn Silverstone mentioned you,' I said.

'Hah, Marilyn! I was with her in Tezpur when the Dalai Lama came. Fine, fine! Now let us sit down. Movement is essential sometimes, stillness is essential sometimes. Tell me your plans.'

I launched into a long mournful tale. He listened, unaffectedly tucking his feet under himself and tapping his knee with his fingers. His gold-rimmed spectacles caught the light. I watched him as I talked. I have a little game I play with people, which in my nastier moments I am proud of: I take notes of their mannerisms, chuckling to myself. I was just starting the first invisible chuckle when I noticed Das chuckling too. His eyes rested on me, intelligent, sardonic, and seeing. I stopped taking notes hastily.

'All is solved,' Das said. 'Ajit K. Das has solved your problem. Come with me to Sikkim.'

'Sikkim?'

'What is education coming to? You have not heard of Sikkim?'

'Yes, of course,' I said stiffly, 'but it's inaccessible, isn't it?'

'Inaccessible? Hah! You leave that to Ajit K. Das. He knows. See, the Chinese are on the Sikkim border. The rumour is that Indian troops are moving in. It is a wild place, with beautiful scenery. We can go up to the Tibetan border. Even if you go to Assam now, it will be raining like hell, and you will not be allowed to go into NEFA for security reasons. In Sikkim you have everything that you have in Assam, and better weather. Also more poetic. Will you come?'

'Yes,' I said.

'Hah! Good. You are a real good boy. Leave everything to me, I will arrange. Only meet me tomorrow morning at seven o'clock at the air terminal. I will fix it up.'

'Tomorrow?' I said weakly.

'Tomorrow. How long you want to stick in this damn place?'

'Oh, all right,' I said.

'Very good. We go to Sikkim tomorrow. Cable your relatives and dependents saying that you are in the care of Ajit K. Das. That will stop them worrying.'

He bounced out again. I fingered my typewriter. It worked. I got a little of my breath back. I decided I liked Ajit K. Das very much indeed.

Later, Galway called. 'Bose wants us to meet some students. And he's fixed up for some writers to call at his flat this evening for us to meet.'

'I'm going to Sikkim tomorrow.'

'Sikkim? A bit wild, isn't it?'

'Yes,' I said. 'When do you leave Calcutta?'

'This evening, after Bose's party.'

'What about these students?'

'Oh, Bose has it all fixed. We have to go to the university.'

So we took a taxi to the university, which is a little way from Chowringhee. A young man was waiting for us at the gate. He took us through a large entrance porch cluttered with grubby marble busts of previous principals to a small room where four other young men were waiting, sitting at a table, thin, intelligent-eyed, and a little spotty.

'These are some of the officials of the Students' Union.'

I remembered a few of the things I had heard about Calcutta students. The Bengalis, and especially the Bengali students, have always been the most vocal, the most intelligent, and the most anarchistic section of Indian society. Their resistance to the British in India was long and vociferous: one result was the caricaturing by Anglo-Indians of the Bengali Babu as always full of ideas he did not understand. The resistance came to its peak when thousands of students took part in anti-British riots. The spirit of revolt engendered then has not yet died down. A month before I reached Calcutta there had been further riots there: bombs had been thrown, and several people killed, including a policeman whose head was cut off. The authorities, alleging that the riots were instigated and organized by the students, had arrested many, and at more than one point had opened fire on crowds of student demonstrators. Who actually did instigate and organize the riots had not yet been proved.

Nevertheless the students of Calcutta are not orderly as students. They tend to go on strike, and not always reasonably. Bose, who is a professor of comparative literature at Jadhavpur University, had complained about their behaviour.

'There is a Spanish Jesuit teaching at the university,' he said. 'One day when the students were on strike, they surrounded him. They called him a dirty Catholic, and they pulled his beard.'

He added, 'The students who broke the strike were assaulted and abused. My own daughter was attacked. They are not disciplined at all.'

So when Galway and I sat down with these students, the leaders of the students of Calcutta, we were neither of us predisposed to like them.

'Can you tell us,' I asked, 'about the part that the students here played in the recent riots?'

'We will have to go into causes,' one of the young men said, 'before we can go into effects.'

He began to detail the grievances of the students against the food minister of West Bengal.

'We are after all interested in the country we are going to inherit. Food distribution is Bengal's main problem. In the old days Jawaharlal would have protested for us. But he has become too old and too entrenched in his position to protest for anybody. Therefore we marched to protest peacefully to the ministry. As we reached it, the police lathi*-charged. Five hundred students were arrested. Forty were killed in the firing that followed. Forty are still missing. More than a hundred are in hospital. At this very moment we are busy drafting petitions for the release of those arrested, and organizing funds for their defence. They have been held without trial for beyond the statutory term.'

'That's all very well,' I said. 'What about the ambulances that were burnt by the students? What about the bomb throwing? And the acid-bulbs? And the policeman whose head was cut off? And the assaults on students who broke the strike?'

'Any demonstration of this kind naturally draws hooligan elements. Our demonstration in the beginning was peaceful.

* Baton.

If the police had not charged us and fired on us the hooligan element would have had no excuse to do what they did.'

'But if this sort of demonstration naturally draws hooligan elements, why hold it? You must know the probable consequences. Why not do it some other way?'

'What other way?' one of the young men said bitterly. 'All the heroes of revolution in India have turned into pillars of the Establishment. Nobody would listen. It is the country we shall inherit, but if we draft a petition, the petition of the inheritors is put into a file by a government clerk and forgotten. If we are to gain anything, we must risk being associated with hooligan elements. If the government had not fired on us, why should they treat us like this now—gaoled, shot, held without trial, lying in hospital after police beatings, unable to speak for ourselves because we are already condemned? Is that part of the process of democracy?'

They kept repeating, bitterly, that there were no leaders in India any more. One of them quoted a line from Buddhadeva Bose to prove it. As intelligent students ought to be, they were familiar with the poets of their time and place, and the first quotation touched off a stream of others from Datta, Chakravarty, Dey, and Samar Sen.

Just before we left I asked what their political beliefs were. They were all Communists.

There was another quiet evening at Bose's flat, where six grave young poets had congregated to read their poems. They treated Bose with a reverence that differed widely from the attitude of young poets in England towards older poets. At the same time it must have been rather irritating for Bose: they treated him like something venerable and fragile: solicitously they plied him with his own whisky. The actual reading was much of a muchness, save that one poet read out a section of the *Iliad* which he had translated into Bengali. Aurally this was a successful translation.

The poet was a small man, with a thin voice, but when he read the poem took hold of him and the room filled like a shell with the murmur and thunder of the sea.

Bose read some of his own poems in the same incantatory whisper in which he had previously read Tagore to us. He seemed self-absorbed this evening, moulding a long hand over his forehead and staring out of the window. But when we left he stood up, taking my hand in both his. 'Come back to Calcutta,' he said, with a charming smile. We had arranged to do some translation together from the Bengali. 'You can't translate Bengali in Chelsea. You will *have* to come back to Calcutta.' With a mischievous giggle: 'Also there is no way back into India from Sikkim except through Calcutta.'

'Why are you going to Sikkim?' said one of the grave young poets. 'It is a savage place, and there are no hotels there. You will have to sleep on the pavements.'

They stood in a little triangle and stared pityingly at me. I averted my eyes and said goodnight to Bose again, then to all the rest. The grave forum opened and shut like a fan, letting us pass.

A Mountain People

> 'We dwell in freedom by necessity,
> A mountain people living among mountains.'
>
> —W.H. Auden

I write this in Gangtok. A thin small rain is falling in streets drifted over with mist. Almost my journey has come full circle, since the day I flew away from London, lonely for you. If I stopped thinking, this could be London, except instead of buses, tasselled mules jingle past under the window, prodded into speed by Tibetan muleteers in felt boots and slouch hats, like Western cowboys.

Inauspicious days…they began when we left Calcutta yesterday. I woke at four and drifted through the motions of bathing and dressing before fully waking up: then to the terminal, far too early, and unjustifiably irritable at Das for being late. He arrived exactly on time, bearing in his arms and about his person two movie cameras, a typewriter, a briefcase, and an airbag. His man followed, carrying a trunk and some rolled-up bedding.

I looked at all this, then at my own small case and typewriter. Perhaps I seemed surprised. Das obviously felt he should explain.

'I always provide,' he said, 'for the basic necessities. Among other things I have brought some rugs in case we feel cold on the Tibetan border, a raincoat in case of rain, and a small brass pot for washing.'

I was a little ashamed.

There was the usual long wait. Presently our flight was announced over the loudspeakers. We bundled out, staggering a bit under the weight of Das's basic necessities, to the aircraft. At this point we were intercepted by an embarrassed airline official.

'Sorry, sir. Announcement was not for you, sir.'

'Who was it for, for God's sake?' I said irritably.

'For the crew, sir.'

'The crew?'

'Yes sir. We have lost our crew, sir. We do not know where they have gone.'

We did not argue. We carried our cargo back to the lobby. An hour later a delighted official rushed up.

'We have found the crew, sir. We have put them in the plane.'

So the delinquent crew flew us off, and two hours later landed us at Bagdogra under a glaring sky. The airport sat in the middle of flat plains: green, spotted with buffaloes and a few men: but off to the north a rim of mountains stood, helmeted in cloud. Das indicated them. 'Sikkim is there,' he said laconically, 'and Tibet.' I was as amazed as a child.

It was very hot. We took a rickety bus to Siliguri, where Marilyn had been arrested. Before we left the airport Das pointed out a room on the first floor.

'That,' he said impressively, 'is the room where she was questioned.'

'Dear Marilyn,' I thought, and felt rather like a pilgrim.

We passed the green fields, the buffaloes squelching up from mud-wallows, the groves of bamboo, the pools full of children, and on every side the cool white speargrass wagging a thousand beards in the windless heat. Presently we crossed a wide, rough brown river; a few peasants stood waist-deep in the water, manipulating fishing-lines with idle flutters of the wrist.

'The Teesta,' Das said. 'We follow this river a long way, it comes with us into Sikkim.'

Siliguri was tiny and ramshackle. We got off at the railway station and loaded our things into the bus for Gangtok. This bus takes the mail from Gangtok to Siliguri and back every day, a journey of twelve hours altogether; the remarkable thing about it is that the same driver operates it always. He was bronzed and wiry, a Sikkimese, chain-smoking and a little sulky. He wore a vest and blue Chinese trousers, but when he got into the bus he took his trousers off and hung them neatly on a nail. I asked him why. He replied that the only reason he could see for wearing trousers was that they had convenient pockets in which money could be kept. While actually driving, he said, he had no need of money, therefore no need of trousers. This seemed logical.

The bus itself was a peculiar one. It was long and low-slung, and physically divided into three parts. The front seat, by the driver, where Das and I sat, was first-class; then came a section cut off on either side by yellow-painted iron bars, like prison bars, second-class; and finally a section shared by mail-bags and third-class passengers. The doors were fastened by a kind of peg on the inside. The luggage went on the roof. 'How long does it take to Gangtok?' I asked Das.

'Six hours.'

'And how far is it?'

'Seventy miles.'

'Seventy miles! Are the roads that bad?'

'It is not only the roads.'

'What then?'

'You will see,' Das said darkly.

We began our journey. After we had reached the outskirts of Siliguri the bus stopped, the driver got out, and we waited. The driver's assistant sat among the mail-bags, singing, I chain-smoked, and Das read the papers. Half an hour passed. 'Where is the driver?' I asked. Das asked the assistant. 'The driver has gone for his lunch.'

The driver returned some time later and the journey went on. The mountains rose taller toward us, dappled with cloud-shadow, hairy giants, clouds like wet linen clinging to their shoulders. An hour's driving found us high up, the bus like a mad beetle skidding along a road that wound tightly round the flanks of the mountains. The driver drooped a cigarette from the corner of his mouth and one hand constantly played with the horn. The horn was rather unique: it was apparently operated through the steering-bar, in which there were a number of little punctures, like the holes in a flute, and the driver ran his fingers over these, producing a kind of horrible melody. On one side the road dropped six thousand feet into a narrow valley, where the Teesta, stronger and clearer than in the plains, roared in foam over huge upended boulders and narrow sandbanks. On the other the mountainside rose vertically, bleeding a thick green vegetation out of its clay, great trees crowding for room, exploding ferns, and jammed among them enormous insecure rocks. Every twenty yards a midget waterfall spilled down the mountainside through a pebbled and mossy crevice, slipping at last over the road to drip towards the valley. Also, there were constant little wooden bridges slung over chasms where branches of the Teesta whispered to their stones. Most of the road signs said, *Danger, Bridge Unsafe for Heavy Traffic:* but the driver's foot was firm on the accelerator, and the bridges shook and creaked beneath us as if the bus itself was a great weight of rushing water. Sometimes also the road signs said. *Beware of Falling Boulders,* and indeed the great boulders balanced so precariously overhead seemed likely to fall out of sheer boredom, and bring the uprooted trees and porous clay down in a slow spin upon us. It was two hours of this, the Teesta always ploughing plain-ward away from us on one hand, and the untrembling mountains rising above us on the other, before we made our next stop, at a village sprawled across the mountainside, where a concrete suspension bridge went over the Teesta. Here the road split: one branch went on through the Himalayas to civilized Darjeeling, with its promenade and missionary schools, the other crossed the Teesta into Sikkim.

The village only had one goat-infested street. The half farther up the mountain was where people stayed, two-storeyed tin-roofed shacks with little slotted windows; the lower half was mostly composed of stalls selling fruit and condiments. This was still the Indian side of the border, but the people were all high-cheekboned and slant-eyed; the women selling fruit in the stalls were often young and very beautiful, with rosy cheeks and a shy downturned look of the face.

Two wandering Tibetans came slowly over the bridge, in their felt boots and cowboy hats, their robes kilted to the waist, and pouches tied to their hips in which each carried his private Buddha. All along the bridge down which they came, Tibetan prayer-flags flapped lazily in the wind to warn off the spirits of the dead. The Tibetans came slowly into the village and slouched down the street, bought fruit and sat down on the grass to eat it, coughing and hawking up the pink pulp like consumptives. When they kilted their robes higher one saw the beautiful embroidered linen belts of Tibet, and when they took off their hats, pigtails spilled over their shoulders and turned them in a minute from cowboys to Red Indians.

I was beginning to feel a little nervous; it was clearly wild country into which we were coming, and the mountains on the far side of the Teesta huddled impassably together, forbidding in their community. So I repeated C.'s remark to Das: was it true that one had to sleep on the pavements in Gangtok? I asked. C. had said so.

'That is an interesting remark,' said Das, 'because it only shows that C. imagines that there are pavements in Gangtok to sleep on.' This did not ease my fears.

We left the littered village after an hour or so, the Tibetans sleeping on the grass, the women crying their wares, children weeping, and at the far end of the street a goat trying to make love to a girl.

Then again the mountains, the slow climbing, the descents,

the bends, and always on one side the following and wandering Teesta, and on the other the hairy mountains.

Occasionally we passed people on the road breaking stones, squatting women, beautiful and wild-looking, men with slant sharp features, dying waterfalls and the growing, sprawling vegetation everywhere, forcing itself sometimes through the cracks of the road. Sometimes the road ceased to be road for a mile or so and became a bridle-path, so narrow that the off-wheel was always trembling on the edge of a terrible decision. It was all very muddy too.

We stopped in a town high up in the mountains. It was market-day, and traders had come in from Kalimpong, spreading their wares in the street, cotton and a little grain and food, and, largest of all, there was a sort of sidewalk department store: combs, sand-shoes, cheap fountain pens, plastic teacups and glasses, charm bracelets, shirts, caps, and, strangely, pink silk knickers. 'Is there much of a market for those?' I asked the trader.

He said yes.

'I shouldn't have thought so.'

'Well, they wear them as fancy hats, you see.'

We spent quite a long while here, because it was time for the driver's tea. When we took off again I went to sleep. When I awoke we were passing a Tibetan mule-train: the mules tasselled and decorated, laced lightly together, with the lead mule free, a mirror on his breast, a bell round his neck, the muleteers loping behind. Then again the Teesta, and a bridge: Rongpo, the Sikkimese frontier.

At the far end were the Customs, a modern police station (the only modern building in Sikkim) and a faded blue-and-gold border sign. We drove on, and now we were always climbing.

As we climbed, I saw cultivation in the narrow valleys for the first time since leaving Siliguri. The fat green earth was cut into wedges, parcelled, forced to bear: the wedges turned to terraces, climbing the foothills. In the mountains themselves an astonishing thing was the number of butterflies, thousands of unhealthily vivid scraps of paper struggling in the wind, and birds dressed in red velvet and blue velvet preening like courtiers among the leaves. Also, the branches of every tree were wired together by cobwebs, enormous cobwebs, billowing in wind, festooned with corpses, and one gross spider sensuously fingering the threads. Even the rocks had cobwebs on them, the butterflies hesitated above them, and the birds looked down and squawked. 'Beautiful, eh?' Das said.

The bus drew up at a village called Sinthan, the driver needed more tea. This was again market-day, vegetables and fruit spread over the pavement on horse-blankets steaming with flies: red-spiked lychees, guavas with their chalky flesh, ginger and peppers. Among the traders the Sikkimese women moved, the young pretty ones with their virgin's gait, like clockwork mice, the old ones like trees floating. A few Tibetans paced about, robes flapping laxly, and everyone looked happy and anxious. When we left, the ones I had talked to stood and waved from the unpavemented street.

More climbing; spiders and butterflies; and at last as we came round the bend of a mountain Das pointed ahead. High up on the next mountainside a few houses were strung out, tin-roofed or thatched. Gangtok. As we climbed nearer we passed caravans loaded with wads of yellowish, smelly wool. 'Yak-wool,' Das said. 'They have come through Tibet, through the Chumbi Valley and the Nathu La Pass to Gangtok.' It was dusk, and the caravan bells chinked rhythmically behind us for a long time before they died away.

As we entered Gangtok, the Last Post sounded from the Indian police station.

Talking and Men

'Rain, rain, and the clouds have gathered,
The eight ply of the heavens are darkness,
The flat land is turned into river.
Wine, wine, here is wine!
I drink by my eastern window,
I think of talking and man....'
—T'ao Yuanming (Tr. Ezra Pound)

In the first of day the mist that drifted over Gangtok all night would thin away into cold and brilliant sunlight, and across the far valleys Kanchenjunga come suddenly clear, like a white nail driven into the sky. It presided over the wakings of Gangtok. In the one straight street which forms the town proper the Indian traders peeled the canvas out of their windows ready for the Sikkimese women who minced in to buy vegetables. The Tibetans uncoiled their long bodies from the alleys where they slept, and the proprietor of the puppet-theatre at the top of the street came coughing and blinking out from under the stage and did a few yoga postures to start the day. There was also a mad beggar whose sex was indeterminate under grey rags, who shuffled and blubbered from shop to shop, holding his brass bowl out in the hope of a little breakfast. He could not speak, only weep, and the shopkeepers did not understand that language and would throw buckets of water over him. This happened every morning. Once I gave him eight annas; but he gave it to a little child.

I awoke more or less with the rest of Gangtok. The hotel we were in was the better of the two in the town; but it was more dosshouse than hotel. There were only three rooms, and six people slept in each. Das's bedding turned out to be of the essence, for the hotel provided none; only low pallets set head to head. The other occupants of the room were mostly Tibetans. They slept with all their clothes on and put their knives under the pillow. This alarmed me somewhat. I took my problem to Das, who was rapidly turning into a sort of father-figure.

'A lot of these fellows may be Chinese spies,' Das said. 'They are all certainly thieves. Keep your money in your sock.'

It was very strange to me. The room smelt of yak-butter from many Tibetan pigtails. The ceiling was entirely covered with cobwebs, swarmed through by black spiders which descended on silk threads at night and bit one. Once I took a glass of brandy to bed with me: when I awoke I found the surface of the liquid covered with a small woollen blanket of dead insects. There were also a great many rats who ran over one after dark. In the end I developed a technique. I bought a lot of matchboxes and kept them by me, and when the scurry of a rat came in the dark hurled matchboxes at the noise till it went away. In the morning the floor would be littered with these matchboxes, which I could never bear to pick up. In the morning, too, the single bathroom was full of people strenuously hawking up the accumulated phlegm of the night. The floor was always covered, as a result, with a slippery liver-coloured jelly, and I could never quite face going in.

Instead I would go out and blink at Kanchenjunga and the narrow street, where the mail-bus coughed slightly, waiting to start for Siliguri. Chiranjilal, the man who ran the shop under the hotel, would come out and offer me a cigarette. Our breath clouded in the bright air. 'What news from Tibet?' '

'Arre, sahib, the Chinia are moving troops to the border, a friend came last night from Yatung.' And he would shake his head at Kanchenjunga. 'What will happen to us if the Chinia come?' But then a pretty Tibetan girl would come in to have iodine dabbed on a cut finger and Chiranjilal would brighten. Massaging her hand, while she giggled and covered her mouth coyly, stroking her forearm a little, he would peer back at me, suddenly small and wicked: 'Arre, there are compensations in life after all.'

Our first visitor in Gangtok came on the evening of our arrival. The hotel had a kind of restaurant, a room with four tables and a curtained-off section for illegal coupling. It looked over the street, where after dark the puppet theatre got going. Drifts of people moved towards it, looked and went away. It was always the same show, the same puppets mincing and cackling on the same wooden trestle-stage against the same backcloth peeling a little more each day. Tonje came up from watching it. 'I watch it every night,' he said. 'It is restful to see the same thing every night.'

He was Tibetan by birth, but a naturalized Indian, and he was the only resident correspondent in Sikkim. He was stocky and walked with the swagger that all Indian hill people seem to have: arms swung back like wings, chest out and hips paddling. He wore always an open-necked shirt, a pale blue jacket, and corduroys, and on his head, with that slight touch of absurdity which I think a grateful thing in a person, a cloth cap exactly like that cloth cap with which the poet George Barker used to intimidate barmen in Chelsea. Also he laughed magnificently and very often, all white and gold.

Das had put his dhoti on to be comfortable and sat cross-legged in a chair by the window, gold-rimmed spectacles flashing, laughing his high laugh and drinking much tea. I had ordered a bottle of Sikkimese brandy, which was sweetish and rather awful, so I was drinking very fast, trying to become hazy enough to forget where I was going to sleep. Tonje, who did not drink, nibbled a

Sikkimese cake. He did not smoke either. 'No vices I have,' he said, laughing explosively.

'Hey Tonje,' Das said in that hectoring tone which was too obviously assumed to be less than lovable, 'what about these Chinese?'

'What about them, Ajit sahib?'

'You have filed any stories?'

'I say, Ajit sahib, I will tell you,' Tonje said. 'This place is full of their spies.'

'That I know,' Das said.

'These Tibetan muleteers. Many of them are spies. Many, many. I have discovered,' said Tonje, growing excited, 'they are paid three dollars a word for every message they send back to the Chinese.'

'That is very clever,' said Das. 'Did you get these statistics straight from Chou En-lai? Or do you discuss salary rates with the muleteers?'

'Ha, you only laugh at me,' Tonje said, laughing. 'But,' he said, 'they come to the frontier every day now. Chinese pickets come. Also by night the frontier guards see their searchlights in the Chumbi Valley. And flashlights near the frontier. Thirty thousand Chinese are in the Chumbi Valley, that is what the traders say.' They talked on, while the valley mist dripped through the windows and a religious procession passed in the street, the chanting drowning out the squawks of the puppets below. The mountain people were happy, but where the two journalists talked, a kind of sobriety, a kind of international apprehension, was created. As Tonje spoke of the Chinese manoeuvres on the border, a small ghost came into the room and squinted at us. Preludes, preludes: to what? For what? As the mist thickened in the valleys and the singers went home, and the brandy began to work, I decided I could go to bed. I left them still talking, over frigid cups of tea.

Next morning Das said briskly, 'We must get moving. Movement, movement, that is the thing, to keep moving, hah?'

'Yes,' I said meekly. Das bounced out to find a taxi. There are three taxis in Sikkim. Das returned with one of them, a Land Rover with a blasé Sikkimese driver and a boy, his assistant. 'Now,' he said, 'we go to the police commissioner. He is my good friend.' We went bumping out of the main street and climbed for a while. Above the main town the houses of the Indian officials in Sikkim are strung out across the mountain. The police commissioner lived in one of these. We drove down a dirt track to reach his house. It was guarded by Nepalese policemen, and a huge blowsy Tibetan stood on the verandah, spitting lazily into the rose-trellises. 'An Indian spy,' Das said. 'Good that we also have spies, hah?'

The police commissioner came out to greet us, a large Sikh, handsome as all Sikhs are handsome, and a little drowsy, a little far away. He took us into his drawing room, a large airy room with swords hanging on the wall and athletic trophies on the shelves. Das introduced me, and the commissioner smiled at me sleepily, twirling his moustaches in his fingers with a gentle contented motion. He was very nice.

'You don't mind,' he said, 'if I see one of my men?'

The Tibetan came in, shuffling and holding his slouch-hat in his hands. He smelt, inevitably, of yak-butter.

'When did you come back?' the commissioner said.

'This morning, sahib.'

The commissioner had a map in front of him. He drew it towards him and fidgeted gently with a pencil. As they talked he marked the map with tiny delicate lines. They talked in Tibetan which neither Das nor I could follow, but every now and then Hindi words came in and we understood snatches.

'*Chinia ko dekha, kya?* You saw the Chinese?'

'Sir, yes, sir. Thirty men. One officer.'

'*Kya karthe the?* What were they doing?'

'I didn't follow them, sir. They were going towards Khamba Dzong.'

'Why didn't you follow them?'

'Sir, I was afraid.'

The commissioner gave his gentle tired sigh. Then he said, 'Go to the bazaar. See if you can find anyone who has come in today from Khamba Dzong. If you find him, send him to me.'

'Sir, yes, sir.'

'Come for your money this evening.'

When the Tibetan had gone the commissioner sighed again: 'You cannot trust any of them. They are all liars.'

Das showed him some photographs taken on his last trip to Sikkim. He was gently pleased with them, stroking his beard, and giving a peculiar courtesy-laugh which consisted of murmuring softly 'Ha ha.' Then he clapped his hands, and a servant brought tea, cake, toast, Punjabi rice pastries, bits of omelette, cheese, and so on. Plate followed plate. My stomach, in a strange disorder already, received this somewhat coldly, so I did not catch much of the subsequent conversation.

'These Chinese on the border, commissioner sahib. What about them?'

'There are no Chinese on the border.'

'But we are told….'

'Sala, that is all bazaar-gup. I tell you, sometimes they come there, five or ten, but all they do is fraternize with the border guards.'

'Fraternize in what way?'

'They talk.'

'About what?'

'Arre, they ask our boys how many they are, where they are placed, what they are armed with, and like that. It is only fraternization.'

'And these lights in the Chumbi Valley?'

'I will tell you, that is simply these muleteers; when they lose some mules they take flashlights and look for them in the night.'

'But the searchlights?'

'Arre, these muleteers may be carrying portable searchlights also.'

'What about Indian army troops moving in as reinforcements?'

'There are none.'

'But we hear....'

'There are *no* Indian troops in Sikkim.'

'Oh, well,' I thought, controlling my rebel digestion, 'hadn't we better go?' The same thought had clearly occurred to Das.

'Well, commissioner sahib, we must not waste your valuable time. We shall take our leave of you. One thing, can you give us a pass to Nathu La?'

'Ha, yes, that can be done.'

'Thank you.'

'One thing, if you have your camera.... There is a football match at the school ground this evening.... Gangtok versus Kalimpong. Why don't you take some few photographs?'

'With pleasure, commissioner sahib.'

'I will give you the pass when we meet at the match.'

'Thank you, commissioner sahib.'

We left him, standing tall and indifferent among his policemen in the mist of the Himalayas.

Sikkim is the second of the three mountain kingdoms of the north. Nepal lies to the west; its border with Sikkim is where the yeti does whatever peculiar things it is supposed to do. Bhutan lies to the east, an impassable roadless mass of Himalayan forest. Northward of all three is Tibet.

Sikkim joins Tibet on its northern and eastern borders. There are two passes into Tibet: the Jelep La and the more strategically important Nathu La, to which a jeepable road has been constructed from Gangtok. Until a very little while ago it was far easier to get into Bhutan and Sikkim from Tibet than it was from India. In fact, until the end of the eighteenth century Sikkim was a dependency of Tibet, and its ruler was designated governor of Sikkim. The ruling house is descended from one of the gyalpos or princelings of Eastern Tibet, and the State religion is Lamaism.

Even now the palace, stalked through by Red Hat Lamas clattering their beads, with its carved wooden gates painted red, its devil masks mounted above the doors, and its long plaintive strings of prayer-flags, is what one imagines Lhasa to be like. There is a constant movement, now as always, of Tibetans to and from Sikkim. Through Nathu La, the mule caravans come tasselled and belled to Gangtok, and even into India as far as the trade station of Kalimpong. Then they come back, and the Tibetans buy pink plastic raincoats in Kalimpong, and drape them round their shoulders against the small ceaseless rain of the passes. Lots of them settle in Gangtok and Sinthan; they are called Bhotias. There was a shop opposite the hotel that sold yak-wool and yak-pemmican and Chinese army issue mugs and plates imported from Tibet, run by a Bhotia mother and daughter. They were very nice, and gave me Tibetan butter-tea and tsampa whenever I visited them. Their people had been in Sikkim for a hundred years; they had gone back to Tibet on a visit every year, until the Chinese came.

The Sikkimese are a fierce and independent people, and Sikkim only became a British protectorate in 1890. It passed over to India in 1947, and the Indian government took over the responsibilities that the British had held. That is, they were in charge of the external affairs of Sikkim, and of defence. Such defence as there has been in the past has been entrusted to armed constabulary, and, so to speak, our friend the police commissioner was almost the minister of defence. India, however, has kept discreet tabs on the internal affairs of Sikkim as well, so that although Sikkim has its own government, the public works department, which has built such roads as there are, is staffed and run by Indians, the post office is run by Indians, and there is an Indian political officer who serves as a kind of grey eminence.

The dewan, or chief minister of Sikkim, is also an Indian; he is usually from the Indian Administrative Service, and acts, among other things, as a liaison officer between the Sikkimese ruler and the Indian government. His office is on a hill above a park where a few miserable deer fetched in from the forest nibble at such herbage as grows between the wire-netting of their cages; when the wind turns a strong smell of deer droppings pervades his room.

Later that morning we saw the dewan. He was leaving next day on an eleven-day tour of the northern borders. He was large and pleasant and seemed delighted at the prospect of pony rides and walks up and down mountains and waking at the foot of Kanchenjunga every morning. But he denied that he was going to inspect the border defences. He did not fear Chinese incursions, he said.

'I do not believe that all this border trouble is more than a diversionary tactic. It is an old Communist trick, you know. Three months ago the world was very excited about Tibet. Now next month the case is coming up at the UN. Meanwhile what do the Chinese do? They take Longju, which is in any case disputed ground, they have a few skirmishes, they refuse to accept the McMahon Line, and the whole world gets excited about the Indian borders. Tibet is forgotten. It is very convenient to the Chinese that the world should forget Tibet at this stage.'

'But what about the new Chinese troops being moved to the border? Why should they bother to do that, if it is just diversionary?'

'You know,' said the dewan, 'as to that, the Chinese may be afraid that the Tibetan refugees in India will cause trouble on the borders.'

'But,' I said, 'there are supposed to be thirty thousand Chinese troops between here and Lhasa, and there are only ten thousand Tibetan refugees in India.'

'It may also be,' said the dewan, 'that they want to seal the border so that no more Tibetans can get out. You see, the more Tibetans leave, the worse the reputation of the Chinese government becomes. They have an interest in keeping the Tibetans inside Tibet.'

'What about the Indian troops in Sikkim? If you don't fear Chinese incursions, why move troops in?'

'We are not moving troops in,' said the dewan firmly. 'Have some tea.'

We left with the mist thickening and met Tonje outside the dewan's office. He flung his arms wide in a gesture of love and surprise. 'Ha, my dear friends! It is a pioneer you are seeing before you. I am going with the dewan to Lachen and Lachung. Pathless, leech-infested territory twenty thousand feet above sea level,' he said with relish, quoting from his next dispatch. 'My dear friends, no food is there, even! I will take,' he planned, furrowing his brow, 'some cold rice and bread, and many tins of beans.'

'And a lorry to carry it all in,' Das said coldly. 'Have some sense. If you travel with the dewan you live like the dewan: off the land. Off the fat of the land too, I think.'

'No, no,' said Tonje. 'This is savage country, my dear friend. Tigers,' he said, snarling, 'bears,' lurching slightly, 'and Abominable Snowmen,' and paused, foxed for a suitable gesture. 'Also there is great danger of being shot by the Chinese. I will take my pistol.'

'Do not endanger the lives of your companions in this foolhardy manner,' said Das.

But we left Tonje gesticulating on the steps of the dewan's office, his cloth cap awry, flushed with the perils through which he had not passed.

Das bounced for the remainder of the morning. He had plans for the rest of the day. We would go a little way up the Tibet road and interview some muleteers. 'Movement, hah? That is the chief thing.' Plans to leave Gangtok, however, necessitate passes. Passes are unobtainable of a Saturday. In small dispirited bounces Das lowered his sights to the football match at four.

The school ground (there is only one school) is cut out of the mountainside, near the Indian residential area, quite far from the bazaar. We arrived to find Gangtok society seated uncomfortably in a small pavilion, and the proletariat scattered about the mountainside in a mushroom-forest of umbrellas. It was drizzling and misty, and also very cold. The commissioner stood on the edge of the playing-field furling his beard in the wind.

'Ha, Das sahib. Have you brought your camera?'

Das waggled the apparatus at him, dolefully.

'Sit down,' said the commissioner, and added optimistically, 'it is going to be a fine match.'

We sat down and looked at the field. Multicoloured players were practising with slightly inappropriate violence. A favourite joke seemed to be to kick the ball very hard into the crowd, which brought roars of joy from the mountainside. The commissioner appointed one of his policemen the judge of the best player on the losing side. Then the match began.

It had only lasted a minute when the ball was kicked out of the ground. Since it was a six-thousand-foot drop into the valley, a new ball had to be procured. This took some while. It was eventually fetched. But the game had scarcely restarted when there was a roar of thunder, a thick grey rain swept down the mountains, and total invisibility supervened. This state of affairs continued for an hour and a half. During this time Das went to sleep, I used my hip-flask lavishly, and Gangtok society peered into the haze, occasionally exclaiming, 'Oh, that is very nicely played, sir!' The only thing resembling contact we had with the match proper, however, was when the ball was kicked into the valley, which happened frequently, and a wet referee appeared demanding another. Finally it was announced that Kalimpong had won. The rain cleared. The mountainside, now denuded of spectators, had turned to a waterfall, the playing-field to a lake. Illuminated by an unconfident ray of sunlight, the commissioner presented the trophies to the winners, while Das clicked his camera vigorously in the distance. Finally one small cup was left. The commissioner turned to the judge.

'Well?'

'Sir?'

'Who is the best player on the losing side?'

'How can I say, sir? I could not even see them playing.'

The commissioner roared very gently into his beard, like a peaceable lion. He was not, however, nonplussed. 'I will present this fine cup,' he said, 'to the entire losing side. They were all the best players.'

There was general applause. The commissioner beamed at us. 'You have taken pictures?' he said. 'Good. Have breakfast with me tomorrow, and I will give you the pass for Nathu La.'

So we tiptoed away across the flooded field to find our Land Rover.

When we got back to the hotel we found Tonje in the restaurant, eating and listening ecstatically to a programme of Indian film music wailed over the radio.

'Do you know what I am eating, Das sahib?' he crowed when he saw us. 'Flesh of swine I am eating! A heathen fellow I am!'

'I am not a Mohammedan,' Das said.

'But I am coming to say farewell to you both, my dear friends, for all our lives,' he said sadly, and then burst into high-pitched giggles. Das scowled and went up to change into his dhoti. He had had a rough time at the football.

Dusk was coming, and apart from the radio everything was quiet and misty. Gangtok breathed softly after the rain. Suddenly a mob of people galloped through the bazaar, doubled forward and with lips pursed as though each was chasing a thistledown. They turned at the top of the bazaar and came charging back in the same way. I looked at Tonje in surprise.

'Some poor bugger has just died,' he explained with a happy laugh. 'But what are all those people doing down there?'

'When a poor bugger dies,' said Tonje, 'the mourners,' he described a mourner with one hand, 'become very frightened of the ghosties.'

'The ghosties?'

'Evil spirits. Yes. The evil spirits come to take the soul. So these mourners make fat their cheeks, so, and they run in the street very fastly, and they go phoof! phoof! and thus the ghosties go away.'

The mourners ran up and down the length of the bazaar seven or eight times, and then ceased their activities. The puppet-theatre began its nightly performance. The mist smoked up from the valley, and I sent a boy for a bottle of Sikkimese gin.

'You should not drink so much,' Tonje said reprovingly. 'You will become an alcoholist.'

Das returned and we ordered dinner. The food was a mixture of Chinese and Bengali, all cooked in a pervasive kind of oil. I was surprised to find myself enjoying it till I remembered that my last meal had been the previous morning.

'Why you don't come to the north with the dewan sahib?' Tonje asked. 'Very interesting for journalists.'

'Too far,' Das said. 'Eleven days.'

'Come up to Dikchu with us,' Tonje said. 'Beautiful country. Mr Dom will write some poetries if he sees that.'

'How far to Dikchu can we go by jeep?'

'By jeep, seven miles. There is a landslide at the seventh mile. Then two hours' walk to Dikchu.'

Das considered, cross-legged, chin in hand.

'Acchcha. We will come.'

'Many Chinia there,' Tonje said gaily. 'We will frighten them away by going phoof! phoof!'

'That is enough of that,' said Das, dourly. 'I go now to sleep.'

Ups and Downs

Next morning we had to have breakfast with the commissioner, and Das insisted on my wearing a jacket and tie. We arrived to find a wiry shrewd-eyed Sikkimese in plain clothes also in the drawing room. He was introduced as one of the border guards. He had just been made an inspector, and we congratulated him. The commissioner smiled benevolently in the background, accepting his share of it all. He had just got up, and still had on the oil-soaked bandages which the Sikhs wear at night to keep their beards in place.

'We are having, you see, some trouble with the refugees,' he said. 'All the able-bodied Tibetans are offered jobs by the Sikkim government, working on the North Sikkim road. Recently there has been some discontent, they are fighting, really giving much trouble.' He sighed more gently than ever and turned to the inspector. 'I have ordered two constables to help you,' he said. 'If you need more take them. Go today to the road-workers' camp. If you find any trouble there, chalan* two or three of them. Nothing stops trouble quicker than a few chalans. And tell the others that those we have arrested will be sent back to Tibet. That will stop all the fuss.'

'Is that not a big decision to take,' Das said, 'to send them back?'

'Arre, the police are always justified,' smiled the commissioner.

---

* Arrest.

Das changed the subject. He turned to the inspector with his most professional, most dentist-about-to-extract-a-tooth-ish smile.

'So you come from the border?'

'Ji ha.'*

'Do the Chinese come to Nathu La?'

The inspector hesitated and looked at the commissioner who was busy unbandaging his beard. He found no help in those calm eyes. 'Ji ha,' he said.

'How many at a time?'

'Sir, most days five, never more than ten. They are only patrols.'

'How often?'

'Every day, sir, sometimes in the morning, sometimes in the evening.'

'Ha!' said Das. 'How are they armed?'

'Sir, with sten guns. But,' said the inspector, getting into his professional stride, 'they have old-type sten guns, with wooden butts like this.'

'And our boys have what?'

'Sir, rifles only.'

'This is a fine state of affairs, hah?' Das said excitedly to the commissioner. 'They have automatic weapons and we have only rifles. What will happen if they decide to attack one fine morning, hah?'

'We have applied,' said the commissioner placidly. 'We have applied for automatic weapons. But the government does not send.'

'Krishna Menon again,' Das said bitterly. 'Defence ministry. All our sten guns are rotting in the plains and here we have nothing.'

'Sir,' said the inspector with dignity, 'we are policemen, it is not our business to carry sten guns.'

'But you're doing army work,' I said, 'at least at the moment.'

---

* Yes, sir.

'That is true,' the inspector admitted. 'But,' he qualified, 'their sten guns have a range of one hundred and fifty or two hundred yards. Our rifles have a minimum range of three hundred but they go up to four hundred. Even to five hundred,' he said rather recklessly.

'Still,' said Das, 'a sten gun is a sten gun, and a rifle is a rifle.'

'True,' said the commissioner profoundly. He wagged his head.

'But,' said the inspector, 'our boys are good shots, and they know how to fight in the mountains. These Chinia do not even know how to hold their sten guns properly. Some are boys of fourteen and fifteen. They don't even have proper uniforms,' in a tone of contempt. 'Some are coolies straight out from China and they go in rags, like coolies. These Chinia can give sten guns to anybody, but they cannot make anybody a good soldier.'

He wrinkled his mouth with disgust, remembering.

'They are cowards as well. When a picket of five come to the border, three advance, an officer and two men; the other two stay behind covering our boys with their sten guns. And we go up to them unarmed, we are not afraid. They are women, sahib.'

'What do they talk about?'

The inspector suddenly revealed unsuspected histrionic ability. He imitated a soldier clutching a sten gun and said in a falsetto voice: 'What are you doing here?'

Then in his own deep voice, holding out empty hands: 'What are you doing here?'

'We are defending our border against aggression.'

'So are we.'

'How often do you come here? How many are you?'

'We come here every day.'

'Don't you have automatic weapons? Who is your general?'

'And like that, sahib,' said the inspector, with a gesture. 'Also, to prove that they are cowards, I will tell you that one reason they have not yet come into Sikkim is that they are afraid of wild animals.'

'*What?*'

'It is true, sahib. All the border guards know this. On their side, in the Chumbi Valley, they have few wild animals. On our side *we* have tigers and panthers and bears. They are very frightened of them. They always ask us have we seen any, are they very fierce, and like that. They are *very* frightened.'

'What do you say when they ask you?' I inquired.

'Sahib, we say that the tigers of Sikkim are the fiercest in the world, and that around the border they eat three men every night.'

He laughed charmingly.

'Each one of us border guards will eat three hundred in one night, when the Chinia come.'

After breakfast we rushed to the post office in the Land Rover: Das wanted to file some dispatches, and I wanted to send you a telegram. 'We must move quickly,' Das said. 'We must get to the seventh mile ahead of the dewan's party, so that I can take photographs. Come, come, come,' he said, whirling me into the post office. 'No gossip, Babuji,' he said to the postmaster. 'We are in a hurry.'

The driver and his assistant entered into the spirit of the thing with terrifying whole-heartedness. The North Sikkim road is a dirt track, clambering through gorges and ravines, and occasionally fording waterfalls, high over rock-strewn valleys. The driver chain-smoked his way along this dubious route at forty miles an hour, and in the back of the Land Rover the assistant, clutching Das's movie and still cameras to his bosom, giggled joyfully and shrieked him on. Das and I, sharing the front seat with the driver, attached ourselves to the struts and bounced for dear life. At last, where many little landslips had littered the track with fragments of rock, clay-heaps, and uprooted plants, and each new bounce took us tilting to the edge, the driver took his foot off the accelerator. The Land Rover shuffled through the debris, bumping still, but less hazardously. Occasionally it had to stop to make room for mule-files. It was during this part of the journey that Das suddenly grabbed my arm. 'Look!' he cried, like Saint Paul.

When I looked farther up the track, shrouded in mist where it climbed the mountain, I saw what I took to be another mule-caravan. But Das had already leapt out of the jeep, and, followed by the boy with the cameras, was sprinting to a rock at the edge of the road. Then as the lead mules came towards us out of the mist, I saw that their packs did not contain yak-wool, borax or herbs, but mountain-guns; and their drivers weren't Tibetans, but Sikh soldiers with rifles, their faces tired and fixed. More and more mules came down the mountain past the Land Rover, some carrying mountain-guns and ammunition, some camouflage-nets, others stores and clothing. And after and among them came the Sikhs, all carrying rifles and ammunition, cocking an eye at Das, who precarious on his rock was furiously working the movie camera. After the Sikhs came Gurkhas, their steel helmets swathed in netting, festooned with leaves and twigs, like many ungraceful Daphnes. There must have been five hundred troops and fifty mules. All through their slow passage Das stylized it on his rock, handing one camera down to the boy while he used the other, and occasionally bestowing delighted winks and salutes upon the passing troops. When they had finally passed, he leapt off the rock and came cantering back, reloading his cameras as he came. 'Quickly, driver,' he shouted. The boy tumbled in at the back as the Land Rover bumped away. Das dexterously reloading his cameras between bumps, yelled in my ear: 'We have beaten the world!'

'Why?'

'Indian troops in Sikkim! They may deny and deny, but we have seen them with our own eyes,' smacking his spectacles. 'We are the first civilians to have seen them!'

He yelled to the boy: 'Look behind, bahadur sahib, great general, and see if the dewan sahib's jeep is coming.'

We arrived at where a waterfall struck the road, bounced, and fell steeply into the rocky valley. As the Land Rover wheezed among boulders and water the boy shouted. We turned. Behind us the track followed the deep inward curve of the mountain, and at the far end of the curve a small train of jeeps was crawling jerkily towards us.

'Shabash, O beloved of the world!' said Das, and precipitated himself into the torrent.

I followed him. The waterfall on our right rushed smoothly down, like a white wall, exploding as it hit the track, and spray rained on us, while the swift water, freezingly cold, tugged at our knees. My position was a little worse than Das's, who, mounted on a rock above the torrent, was madly working the movie camera as the jeeps inched round into the curveway. Then he leapt off the rock and we both squelched back into the Land Rover.

'Chalo, chalo,' I said, catching Das's mood. 'Drive on!'

'Sahib, injin bundh hua,' said the driver gloomily. 'The engine is dead.'

'Then we must push,' Das said invincibly, and out we tumbled again.

Pushing a Land Rover through a waterfall is not easy. For one thing, we had to keep lifting boulders out of the way. For another, when we got into the middle the current was so strong that it flattened us against the car and shifted that a little farther towards the edge. All this while the dewan's procession was closing in on us from behind.

We managed somehow. As we dripped up on to reasonably dry land behind the Land Rover the engine coughed a little and began working. Das, the boy, and I fell into the back and we pulled away as the dewan reached the waterfall.

Das's camera was busy again. He knelt wetly and bucketingly in the back, shooting away as the dewan's jeep started fording the waterfall. It was much quicker about this than ours had been. Soon we found ourselves the leader of the cavalcade by about twenty yards.

'Scoop, scoop, scoop,' Das kept saying gleefully. I was so wet I didn't care.

Finally we reached a little village of thatched and tin-roofed huts spread down the mountain towards a valley now cross-hatched with cultivated fields. The villagers were lining the road with scarves and garlands, the prayer-flags fluttering in the thin mist overhead. Under the impression that we were the dewan, everybody began to salute and advance with the garlands. Das promptly rose and bowed. As we pulled up, however, the real dewan arrived. Tonje tumbled out of one of the jeeps behind him and came rushing through the mud, also with a movie camera.

Das hopped out too and they both levelled their lenses at the emergent dewan, like the nozzles of sten guns. The dewan wore his State clothes: a brown jacket buttoned at the neck, and jodhpurs, in his hand a sandalwood stick. He accepted the garlands and scarf-offerings and returned them with a gracious gesture. Then he walked with dignity to the edge of the road, accompanied by his entourage, and they all peed into the valley. Tonje and Das stopped their cameras hastily, and we joined ranks on the edge. Finally the dewan buttoned his trousers, and stood gazing seignorially at the village, as if in thought, gently tapping his leg with his stick. Then he climbed back into his jeep. We all scrambled for our respective jeeps, doing ourselves up as we went, and the cavalcade began afresh. The road was worse here. The landslip ahead had precipitated other minor landslips, and the track was flooded in many places and sputtered over by newly created waterfalls. When we reached the big landslip I felt inured, but even so was startled by what I saw. The entire mountain seemed to have caved in, leaving raw fissures in the slopes, and a kind of dwarf mountain had been created on the track: earth, rocks, and uprooted trees upside-down in the debris, while water flooded through.

The entire cavalcade drew up, and everybody got out and stood peering at the landslip. 'Is it safe to cross?' the dewan said.

'On foot, yes, sir,' said the private secretary, who wore leather shorts and a peaked cap. The porters with the dewan's baggage appeared labouring along in the Sikkimese manner, with their packs fastened by a strap round their foreheads. They began to negotiate the landslip, while the dewan poked it experimentally with his stick. Then we all climbed over. It was all right, save for one horrible moment, when, balanced on the slippery clay at the top, I looked down at the rocks of the valley three feet across from my right shoulder and several thousand feet beneath my right toe. Now we straggled through forest mud. Tonje, huffing and puffing under his camera, was my companion. Das galloped about the mountainside ahead, unbelievable in his energy, taking photographs. It took about two hours to get to Dikchu, a small high village, mist-wrapped and cold, and by that time even Tonje was speechless. Das still limped beside the dewan, taking notes. The villagers came out, did obeisance, and showed us to a collection of pallets outside the headman's hut. Here we sat down and were brought Sikkimese tea, which is mostly hot milk, and buckwheat cakes. It came on to rain. Presently Das rose. 'Good luck, dewan sahib,' he said. 'We go now back.'

Tonje saw us to the edge of the village with effusive goodbyes. 'Perhaps I may never see you again, my dear friends.'

'One can always hope,' Das said ambiguously. He was a little embittered by exertion. The villagers sent a boy with us as guide.

Das and I squelched back for two hours through ever-increasing rain. It was nearly dark by the time we reached the Land Rover, dumbly faithful at the far side of the landslip. The driver and his assistant were both asleep. We woke them and began our journey back in silence and very nearly in tears. I kept discovering leeches in my clothes. Das was too tired to worry about leeches.

We got back to the waterfall where we had stuck, and stuck again. We were knee-deep striving when a mule-caravan jingled up. The muleteers stood akimbo on dry land urging us to hurry. At length they were tired of waiting, and decided to try to take the mules across on the far edge. Four mules went over safely. The fifth stumbled in the stream and abruptly disappeared. There was a shriek like a woman's, and a heavy crash far below. The muleteers peered over the edge of the cliff, clicking their tongues. The mule had fallen about a hundred feet; and been brought up short by a boulder. It lay now straddling the boulder and heaving as if trying to bring something to birth. The mirror on its breast had splintered, and the tassels been torn away. It looked curiously nude without them, and blind, struggling against what it could not see. Thick mud-coloured blood dripped from its side.

Two of the muleteers took their knives out of their silver scabbards and began very cautiously to climb down to the mule. It was like a sacrifice, the animal on the mountain, mute and struggling to be comfortable, and the knife-carriers descending to it. But the Land Rover was now across, and we drove away.

We did not reach Gangtok till midnight. Das had fallen asleep and it was an effort to wake him. I was very tired, and aching and itching all over from bumps and leeches. I tried to think of you, but my mind was too tired to function. All night I could not sleep.

Tibetans from Tibet

'… existence is believing
We know for whom we mourn, and who is grieving.'
—W.H. Auden

Next morning Das said proudly, 'We may have overexerted, but still we have scooped the world, hah? We have films of the first Indian troops in Sikkim.'

'Good show,' I said idiotically.

'Now we shall go and see the PO,' Das said. 'He may be having some hot story.'

As we went down to the Land Rover Chiranjilal came out of his shop. 'Hey, Ajit sahib,' he said, 'the press attaché has been telephoning for you.'

'Now what does that raper of his mother want?' Das wondered agreeably. He went into Chiranjilal's shop to telephone. I talked to the driver and his boy.

The driver lolled back across the seat, a cigarette in his fingers, speaking in small blue puffs.

'You go to Nathu La soon?'

'Tomorrow or the day after.'

'I see no reason for it. It is a wild place. Yaks and savages live there, not civilized people like we have in Gangtok.'

The boy said: 'Also the Chinia are on the pass with guns.'

'Silence, boy,' said the driver. 'However,' he said, 'your friend the journalist may be interested in going tomorrow. Chhibar sahib is coming.'

'Who is Chhibar?'

The driver looked shocked. 'The Indian consul in Lhasa. He comes out tomorrow.'

'How do you know?'

'A friend of mine came from Yatung today. He passed Chhibar sahib's mule caravan. Chhibar sahib was in Yatung last night. He is spending today in Yatung and tomorrow morning he comes to Nathu La.'

At this point Das returned. His face was as sorrowful and angry as Saint Sebastian's.

'Imagine what those sons of bitches have done!' he moaned, climbing into the Land Rover. 'A government order to confiscate my films of the troops!'

'Surely they can't enforce it?'

'Arre, if I do not give in, they will never let me into Sikkim again. Those sons of bitches! Why are they frightened that the world should know? Two hundred feet of film,' he mourned, 'at sixteen rupees a hundred feet,' and another arrow seemed to whiffle home.

I tried to think of healing ointments. 'The driver says the Indian consul in Lhasa is coming out through Nathu La tomorrow.'

'Hah?' exclaimed Das. 'What is that?' He leant forward and began to cross-examine the driver. Finally he leant back with a small complacent smile. 'On this then,' he said, 'we shall beat the world.' He thought deeply, then looked up, beatific. 'Let us go now to the PO.'

The grey eminence, the political officer, Mr Pant, lives in a beautiful gardeny house on a hill-top. Pant is one of the best of the younger Indian diplomats. He was high commissioner in Nairobi during the Mau Mau troubles, is an expert on India's northern frontiers, and has visited Lhasa during the Communist regime. He is very tall and extremely handsome, with eyes that seem hooded and inward like the eyes of Nehru.

Now he received us in what, even without comparison with our own hotel, was a truly gracious-living sort of drawing room ('it makes you afraid to tread on the carpet, hah?' Das murmured) and offered us tea. Then he took a quick hard look at me and said with unflattering perception: 'Would you prefer some beer?'

'I would indeed,' I said enthusiastically. The beer was brought. It was very good, very cold Danish lager. I drank it and looked at the mist troubling the grass and smoked Mr Pant's Turkish cigarettes and felt happy. Occasionally, I scraped a little moustache of foam off my upper lip and listened to what Das was saying to the PO. He had launched into a long diatribe about his film. Mr Pant listened gravely.

'We can't let you release it, you know,' he said, shaking his head. 'I'm sorry, but we really can't.'

Das sputtered, and then with the true journalist's imperturbability began his questions.

Mr Pant was amiable and historically informative. 'Longju, after all,' he said, 'has always been disputed territory. The British mapped it as an unsettled part of India, that is, they collected no taxes there, they had no district officer, and so forth. On the other hand, the Tibetans have collected taxes there off and on over a long period. Since 1947 the Indian government has been collecting taxes there and making roads and that sort of thing, but it is disputed territory. The same with most of the other areas where the Chinese have moved in. We cannot say with authority that they have always been an integral part of India.'

Sometimes he became very acid. 'Don't you think,' Das said, 'that you should let me write that there are Indian troops in Sikkim? It might also warn the Chinese that we are prepared.'

'Do you think,' said Mr Pant, 'that they don't know? Do you think five hundred words in the *Indian Express* by Mr Das will send the Chinese running all the way from Nathu La to Peking?'

I intervened at this point. 'Do you think they will attack India?' I said rather crudely. 'After all, that's what it's all about!'

'This year, no,' said Mr Pant. 'If you were to ask me that next year, I don't know what I should say.'

He hooded his eyes at me and said in his beautiful deep voice: 'You are the poet.'

'I suppose so,' I said.

'Let me see what I can remember from the newspapers.' He closed his eyes. Then they opened again. 'You were at Oxford!' he said accusingly.

'Yes,' I said.

'So was I,' said Mr Pant delightedly. 'What college were you at?'

For the next half hour we wandered over Oxford, the grey stones wedged together with books, the bicycles, the Epstein in New College chapel, the dons like huge fruit-bats flitting through the dusk to the Hall. Das brought us out at the other end on to a dry table land of no nostalgia.

'Is it true, Apa sahib,' he said a little impatiently, 'that Major Chhibar reaches Nathu La tomorrow?'

Mr Pant looked irritable again. 'Who told you that?' He had Nehru's imperiousness as well as Nehru's eyes.

'Ah,' said Das in modest triumph. 'I have my sources.'

'Yes,' said Mr Pant, and I congratulated the taxi driver in my heart.

'At what time this will be?'

'He's supposed to get there at eleven,' Mr Pant said.

We wished one another cordial goodbyes. 'You talked so much,' Das said fretfully as the Land Rover took us away, 'I was not able to get a word in sideways even.'

Later in the morning we drove up the North Sikkim–Tibet road to inspect progress. The engineer in charge, a slim hairy man, came with us. We started on the same road along which we had come the previous day, but at the fifth mile branched off to the north.

The new road is cut high up on the mountainside. On one hand, the bald rock rose three hundred feet through the clouds, on the other, birds hung above immense gorges, cluttered with trees and veined with the silver blood of streams. Tibetan work parties sat phlegmatically chipping stones at intervals along the road. Little flocks of shanties pimpled the slopes. 'The labour camps,' said the engineer. 'We provide well for these refugees.'

The road as yet is a dirt track. About fifteen miles of it have been cut, but when it is finished it will be sixty miles long, leading to the North Sikkim–Tibet border. We went about ten miles. The first five were the easiest; then came the usual landslips, waterfalls, and, most terrifying, points where the road was only just wide enough to take the Land Rover, a thread on the shoulder of the mountain hung over the tree-packed valley. The driver smoked with one hand and drove with the other, occasionally I closed my eyes. The engineer pointed this out to Das and they both laughed happily.

We stopped at last by a work party clearing the debris of a landslip. They were Tibetan refugees, girls and men with brown mountain-lined faces, the exact colour and texture of sea-sand. They looked at us curiously. Das began to work the movie camera, and I wandered a little way up the road. There were butterflies everywhere, struggling from the foliage and the rocks and drifting off sideways to float over the valley. At one point, by a bed of straggling purple flowers, there were so many that they settled all over me, as in the legend of the prince. The undergrowth by the road smelt wet and herbal: to breathe this tart chill air was like biting into an unripe apple.

I came back to find Das had finished and was ready to go back. There was a tractor farther down the road and he wanted to film it in operation. 'Let us take some of these fellows with us,' he said, 'for local colour.'

So a dozen Tibetans piled into the back of the Land Rover, Das, the engineer and myself piled into the front, and we started back.

It was not a restful journey. The weight of the men in the back was unequally distributed. On the fly-walk above the gorge they canted the Land Rover over so that often it balanced on two wheels on the extreme edge. Vertigo had a queer physiological effect on me. The splayed paintbrush of each tree in the valley seemed to daub my eye with green: by the time we stopped the tractor my vision was completely green, like a mad camera: even the Tibetans had green faces. It took some time for this to wear off. I sat in the Land Rover composing myself while the engineer, perched high in the cockpit of the tractor, incited it to snort and heave in a baffled way. The Tibetans meanwhile stood sadly around. I wanted to talk to them.

'Tibeti janthe ho?' I asked the driver. 'Can you speak Tibetan?'

'Ese ese,' he said, which is Hindi for cosi-cosi.

I beckoned two Tibetans over. They were father and son, I think; they wore ragged blue trousers and vests instead of robes but they retained their slouch-hats. They smiled uncertainly at me and were silent.

'Tell them,' I said, 'I hear there is some trouble among the road-workers here. Ask them what it is.'

He asked them. They hesitated, then the younger one brought forth the flat smacking Tibetan consonants. He went on for a little while and stopped, waiting to be translated, his tongue thrust politely between his lips.

'He says they do not like it here. They do not get paid enough, they have not enough time with their families. He says this is not the work they want to do.'

The engineer had now produced a definite result. The tractor screamed and began to struggle down the road, Das trotting behind with his camera. I had to shout to make myself heard.

'What do they want to do?'

After a short exchange: 'He says in Tibet they are farmers.'

The older Tibetan now chipped in. He had to shout too, opening his mouth wide, revealing blackened teeth and a black lizard's tongue. His eyes were anxious, pleading like a bulldog's through wrinkled folds of skin.

'He says nobody understands their language here. He says he finds it hard at his age to become a foreigner.'

'Ask him if he wants to go back home.'

Presently the driver said: 'He says he has lost his home. His home is in the country where the Dalai Lama stays, but he is not at home here. If he goes back to Tibet now the Chinia will shoot him. His brother went back and him the Chinia took and shot.'

'But if he doesn't want to stay here and doesn't want to go back, what *does* he want to do?'

A short translation and the old Tibetan began his answer. He spoke with the same strange naturalness which had been the dignity of the Alakirti Lama in Kathmandu. The younger man shook his head in agreement. The tractor had stopped and Das was now taking still pictures.

'He says he wants to be back in Tibet before the Chinia came, when the Dalai Lama was in the Potala and the Tashi Lama at Shigatse, when he lived with his brother and their wife north of Lhasa. He wants those days to come back. He says why does India not drive the Chinia out of Lhasa? He says his people are fighting, and if India does not help they will all die.'

In the heavy silence that followed the cessation of the tractor's screams the old Tibetan and I looked helplessly into each other's eyes. I thought of Hungarian refugees on the Austrian frontier, cloth caps, cloth bags, muddy shoes, and always the same hard painful eyes. I thought of what the Dalai Lama had said in Delhi. 'The poor and dispossessed....' There was nothing I could do beyond what I did, the simple and meaningless compromise, a smile, a touch of the hand.

Only that morning I had never heard of Major Chhibar, but his name wove itself into a litany that was repeated all day, by Das, by Chiranjilal, by the shopkeepers in the bazaar. Chhibar had been three years in Lhasa. During the flight of the Dalai Lama his consulate, from which the first news had been sent to India, had been surrounded by Chinese soldiers. Now he was coming back to be the Indian first secretary in Gangtok. He had already been travelling fifteen days from Lhasa, through Gyantse, Yatung, and the Chumbi Valley, and the bazaar was full of reports from Indian traders coming back: that Chhibar had been detained by the Chinese in Gyantse and his diplomatic luggage searched, that the Indian traders in Yatung had appealed to him for protection.

Bazaars are good places for picking up news. Das wandered about while I sat with my friends, the Tibetan mother and daughter, in the back of their shop, drinking butter-tea, eating small pieces of dried yak-meat and flirting a little, to make myself feel younger, with the daughter, who was pink and pretty and giggled all the while, her knuckles to her lips. Das returned in the midst of all this, with a whole notebook filled with information and a cross look.

'That son of a bitch of a taxi driver wants three hundred rupees to take us to Nathu La. Have you ever heard such dung?' He sat down beside me and flumped his hands down on his knees, sitting four-square and rigid with indignation, as always when deeply moved.

'How far is it, though?'

'Thirty-five miles there and thirty-five back. Seventy in all. It is true that the roads are bad,' said Das, 'also we climb all the time, but three hundred rupees is a damn cheek.'

'Well, but who else is going to take us?'

'I have hired a jeep for a hundred and fifty,' Das said. 'It is outside now.'

So I went out and looked at the jeep. It was decrepit in the extreme.

'There aren't any waterproof door-covers,' I said as a preliminary objection. 'We'll get as wet as hell.'

'Those he can put,' Das said. 'Otherwise it is okay, hah?'

I pointed out a more fundamental lack. 'Where is the hood?'

'That is true,' Das said thoughtfully. 'Where is the hood?'

'Sahib,' said the driver, 'that is only a lid. I had to keep lifting it up and down when I wanted to look at the engine. It was too much trouble. Bahuth mushkil hua. Therefore, I removed the lid, and now there is no trouble.'

I know nothing about cars, but it seemed to me that if it rained, as it certainly would, the engine would get wet. I said so.

'No, sahib,' said the driver. 'Many times I have been to Nathu La. Never has there been any trouble. My boy has the heart of a lion, and is a fine mechanic. The best in Sikkim. Also I am the best driver in Sikkim. This is well known.'

'The offside tyre is flat,' I said.

'That he can blow up,' Das said. 'Arre, Dom, tell me, what other jeep would take us at this price? Every item missing means twenty rupees less.'

'Well,' I said, 'if he thinks he can do it....'

So it was settled. Das worked out the times on his fingers.

'Three hours to get to Nathu La. Chhibar is coming at eleven. So he would leave at eight. I have to file some dispatches in the morning. Say seven-thirty. Come at seven-fifteen,' he told the driver. 'Otherwise I will eat your life.'

In the hotel we ordered hard-boiled eggs, a loaf of bread, and a bottle of brandy for the morning, looked at the puppet-show for a little while through the window, and went to bed.

Tibetans from Peking

As usual I woke at five. I woke with a vague thought of hard-boiled eggs and liquor and a feeling that Julian and Del and Ved and I were going for a picnic along the Cherwell. Then I inhaled the foetid air of the bedroom and remembered. I went out on the terrace, shouted for a bucket of water, and splashed for a little. Day had come up over Kanchenjunga and there was a flavour of snow, woodsmoke, and herbs in the sunlight. I dressed and sat on the terrace, drinking brandy, watching the bazaar waking up, and reading *The Memoirs of Hadrian*. I knew when Das got up because his typewriter started raiding away and there were sleepy shouts of protest. At precisely seven-thirty he came out to me. He carried his cameras and typewriter, and, rather depressingly, his first-aid kit.

'Ready? Good. Let us go.'

The jeep had arrived. There was a slight delay while we put in eight gallons of petrol from the shop across the street. Then we drove uphill to the post office, and Das sent his telegrams.

The expedition seemed to have begun. But a hundred yards up from the post office, where the road became steep, the jeep suddenly ceased to work. It roiled gently backwards down the hill and stopped again exactly in front of the post office. The postmaster issued forth in some surprise.

'You want to file another message?'

'No,' said Das grimly, then to the driver, 'Son of a donkey, what has happened to your jeep?'

'Sahib,' said the driver, shamefacedly, 'now it will work.'

He started the engine and we climbed the hill again. At the top the jeep stalled conclusively. Once more we slid gently down to the post office. The postmaster had now been joined by his entire staff. They were laughing.

'Go back to the bazaar, O fatherless one!' Das said between his teeth.

But the engine had died completely. We coasted back under control of the law of gravity. Once in the bazaar, Das jumped out with murder in his eyes.

'Go to Chiranjilal's shop,' he said. 'I will settle with this bastard.'

Chiranjilal was all concern. 'It is five past eight,' he said. 'You will never get there in time for Chhibar.' He began telephoning various people to see if another jeep could be found. It was in vain. At eight-thirty Das returned in a fury.

'This driver has paid me back for the petrol,' he said, 'and I got our old Land Rover. But that driver wants five hundred rupees now.'

'I will talk to him,' Chiranjilal said.

So we all went out, Das, Chiranjilal, the two shop-assistants and myself, to where the driver straddled the front seat of the Land Rover, grinning hugely. A small crowd had gathered, including the Tibetan mother and daughter. Chiranjilal, Das, and the shop-assistants all shouted at the driver together.

The driver continued to grin, and occasionally to breathe smoke into the air, ogre-wise. Otherwise he gave no sign.

'These are very important sahibs,' Chiranjilal said. 'Chhibar sahib wishes particularly to see them. You will gain great honour from the dewan sahib if you take them.'

'My honour has already been taken away by these sahibs,' said the driver. 'I am being generous when I charge only two hundred rupees extra for it.'

'We will give you four hundred,' said Das, almost pleadingly.

'Five,' said the driver, adamant. I looked at my watch. Quarter to nine. Lost, I thought.

At this point the Tibetan mother, at the fringe of the crowd, lifted her beautiful aquiline head and called: 'Shame on you, Sanje, and shame on Sikkim. You should be privileged to do anything for these sahibs. And here you are bargaining for more money to give your unchaste wife for jewellery, and bringing your country nothing but disgrace.'

The driver looked at her, then looked back at us, and said sulkily: 'Two-fifty. Get in.'

I shot our preserver a grateful glance. She returned a broad wink. I laughed with relief. I could have kissed her.

We left Gangtok at about nine.

'Bahadur sahib,' Das said flatteringly, 'if you get us to Nathu La by eleven, we will call you Rajkumar, a prince.'

'Sanje is sufficient for me,' said the driver disagreeably. 'Do you think I have wings to fly to Nathu La?'

I offered him a cigarette, and said guilefully, 'If you get there by eleven, we will pay three hundred rupees.'

'Sahib,' said the driver, suddenly tractable, 'if you say half past eleven, I can do it.'

He sucked tentatively at my cigarette as we climbed out of Gangtok into the Himalayan track.

'It will be raining. There is fog ahead. I will try. Sahib,' he said, looking at the cigarette in his fingers, 'do you make these yourself?'

'They are made by a great sahib in Bilayat,'* I said, 'called Du Maurier.'

'Do you know this sahib?' asked the driver.

'Of course,' I said.

'If he comes to Sikkim,' said the driver, 'recommend me to him. He must be rich. I will take him to Nathu La for a thousand rupees.'

---

* England.

Then we passed into the mist.

Out of the mist, every so often, mules blundered like moths against the headlights. Behind them the tall shivering muleteers raised their arms in salute as we passed. As we climbed that spiral funnel towards the sky, the air thinned and rain began to whip tinily in with a knife-cold wind. I pulled the waterproof across the doorway, cutting off the view and saving myself from vertigo, for the track had narrowed to a strip of mud disintegrating in rain. We passed a huddle of shacks outside which cold policemen stood. 'Karponang,' Das said. 'Twenty-three miles still.' I looked at my watch again. It was ten to ten. 'Good going.'

Das said, 'Last time I passed through Karponang there were ten feet of snow. Mist everywhere also, you could not see even. I was coming back from taking medicine to the first Tibetan refugees, just after the flight of the Dalai Lama. My driver was driving with one hand and telling his beads with the other: he was a Buddhist. But I also thought we were going to die that day.' He hesitated and said: 'One should not bother about dying.'

Cigarettes gave one a strange ill feeling so I stopped smoking and squinted ahead through the mist-frosted windscreen. Only one of the wipers was working; it hissed and snicked to and fro; as a child I used to call them 'Vipers.' Presently we passed a gutted building.

'The old fifteen-mile checkpost,' Das said; 'It burnt down last year. Soon comes the new one.'

Ahead the mountainside widened and accommodated a kind of village with a worn wooden gate and a barbed-wire palisade across the road. A policeman came dripping out in a waterproof to inspect our pass. He took down the particulars, and nodded, unspeaking. We drove on. 'Nine miles to Chhangu.'

For the next half hour we leant slowly, noiselessly, through a cotton-thick mist. Rain fell. It was bitterly cold, and I draped my knees with one of Das's blankets. Then we moved out of the mist, to a cold burning of sunlight, and the unwinding road brought us down to a great lake. The mountains lay, wobbling gently, under the water; the water was powdery and blue, like an eye, like a pearl, and shivered all over by the risings offish.

'Chhangu Lake.'

We climbed again, till we had left the mountain hollow of the lake behind us. Mule caravans were now very frequent. The landscape was changing noticeably. All the way from Gangtok, the mountains had been humped and rough with trees. Now they seemed to have broken off in the air, jagged and pointed, and furred over with thick grey-green lichen, on which broken fragments of limestone lay. Among this lichen browsed enormous antediluvian animals, hung round with black hair, like woollen blankets walking, with horns splaying massively across their low brows. 'Yaks.' The driver pointed out a reddish flower coquetting in the wind. 'Poison-flowers, sahib. You only find them here. Touch, and you die.'

The sunlight burnt on, an icy fever, and wind tacked across the shelved valleys, altering the clouds. We reached another hamlet, another worn gate, more barbed wire. Yaks were browsing between the huts. One raised his great matted head with a deep sleepy bellow.

'Sherathan,' Das said. 'The last checkpost. Two miles to Nathu La. What's the time?'

'Ten past eleven.'

'Not bad. Good. Shabash, driver. Three hundred rupees for you. Chhibar also may be late,' he explained to me.

Now we were climbing all the way, above the blue sockets of two more lakes, anthology of the tears of all the rocks. The landscape had an undated quality, prelapsarian perhaps, and the yaks, shaggy and gentle because their eyes were hidden under hair, might have floundered to Adam's hand in Eden. Ahead, the road became well trained, covered with small slaty flagstones like fish scales. Then coming round a bend we saw it lift, under walls, to where a jeep was parked and three uniformed midgets stood. Das gave a deep sigh of achievement. I looked at my watch. Eleven-thirty. 'That is Nathu La.'

We pulled in at a small shelf cut into the mountain-top, a lichen-rusted hummock rising beyond. The shelf had for ornament a small stone boundary-post, inscribed 'Sikkim-Tibet Border'. Pools of water lay about, memorials of the morning's weather. A police officer and two constables greeted us with a request for our passes.

Then Das and I climbed the hummock, to look into Tibet. The sun had come out brilliantly and coldly, and the sky over Tibet was an icy blue. From where we stood the mountain slipped steeply down, dry and boulder-strewn, into the Chumbi Valley, a succession of folds in the ground, thickly forested, rippling to a narrow V. At the point of the V, across the valley, rose a range of forested hills. Beyond them the horizon was like a picture postcard, two scarred snowpeaks vivid in the frosty sky, and a glimpse of plains between and beyond. The police officer came silently up behind us, pointing out the higher of the snowpeaks.

'That is Chumbiladi.'

'Where does Tibet start?' I asked.

'My dear gentleman,' said Das, 'we are in Tibet. It starts from the boundary-post down there.'

'Where are the Chinese?' I inquired naively.

The policeman handed me his field-glasses. I followed his finger as it swept the Chumbi Valley. Where the valley turned into hills, at the point of the V, I made out a small concrete building among the trees.

'That is their checkpost, at Chumbithan. But who can tell where those rapers of their sisters are? They hide here and there in the jungle and watch us through field-glasses. But I can tell you, sahib, there must be a hundred or two between here and Chumbithan, and that is two miles.'

'Chinia aye the aj, kya?' Das asked. 'Have they come here today?'

'Ji nahin. No, sir. They will not come till Chhibar sahib has passed. This is their diplomacy'.

I turned and looked about. Huge cairns of stones littered the hummock, ominous and druidical. Above them hundreds of improvised prayer-flags, made of tattered garments, tautened in the whipping wind out of Tibet.

'What is all that?'

'When these Tibeti folk come back from Kalimpong or Gangtok they throw a stone at the border, to drive away the evil spirits from abroad. Also they put up those flags for good luck.'

Clouds swept over the sky, and suddenly mist rose everywhere, and Tibet was blotted out of sight as completely as if it had never been there. I could understand, suddenly, why the Tibetans believe that evil spirits live in these high passes. The cairns loomed gloomily; the prayer-flags hung limp, then whiffled in the wind. I found myself strangely exhilarated. 'It's the air,' I thought; then, as the wind sang over the pass, shivered, helpless with cold.

Das, drinking the wind like a tonic, rushed sharply about, posing the policemen, the drivers and myself in various places, against the cairns and flags, drooping over the boundary-post, and so on. He had given me his movie-camera to hold, and that hand had turned completely numb. I tried to talk to the police officer, but it was difficult to move my lips.

However, 'What do you think?' I said. 'Will the Chinese attack?'

'Sahib, that is what their officers tell everybody. The yak drivers and the muleteers say that the Chinese promise to be in Sikkim before next summer.'

'What will you do then?'

'Fight, sahib. What else? Only the sarkar* must give us material for us to fight with. Our radio transmitter here works only three hours a day. If the Chinia should come while it is not working,

* Government.

how can we let them know at Sherathan, so that our boys can be ready there?'

'Well, they can see Nathu La,' I said, 'through field-glasses.'

The police officer laughed.

'Sahib,' he said, 'the garrison at Sherathan has no field-glasses. They have asked for some, but the sarkar does not send. If there is fighting at Nathu La, our men at Sherathan will not see it till the Chinia are on their heads.'

The mist was thinning. He swept the Chumbi Valley with his field-glasses. Then he said, 'Someone is coming.'

I shouted to Das, who returned from his photography at a trot. He peered through the field-glasses, then passed them to me. Four or five men on mule-back were snailing up one side of the valley.

'It doesn't look like a diplomatic party,' I said.

'It may be some traders,' said the policeman. 'Let us wait.' I remembered the brandy. We squatted, all of us, under a cairn, which afforded some protection from the wind, and passed the bottle from hand to hand. Mist went over in little puffs. The brandy had a strange, fiery effect, fifteen thousand feet up: my ears sang and I felt sick.

As the mist lifted again for a minute, we saw the mule-riders plodding up from the foot of the hummock towards us. Das jumped up and shouted for his movie-camera. He began to work it as the first rider reached us. Three others drifted after him. They were definitely Indian traders: small heavily muffled men, with nervous rolling eyes, like apprehensive ponies. The first one dismounted, and Das was at him like a terrier.

'Welcome. Where are you from? Yatung, hah? Kya hal chal hai Yatung me?'

'Bahuth mushkil he Yatung me, sahib. Much trouble. Yesterday the Chinia killed an Indian trader there. Their people stabbed him and looted his shop. Therefore, this morning we left there, closing our shops. There are only three Indian shops open in Yatung today, where once there were fifteen.'

The police officer interrupted. 'Have you seen Chhibar sahib?'

'He was leaving Yatung an hour after we left, inspector sahib. We thought, if we came before, we would be safe; if we came after, the Chinia would eat our lives.'

'So,' said Das thoughtfully. 'He will still be one hour.' He glanced into the misted valley. 'Are there any Chinia down there?'

'Many, many Chinia,' one of the other traders said. 'They are in the forest, three furlongs down the valley.'

'Why don't we go down and look at them?' I suggested.

'That is what I also was thinking,' Das said.

Brandy and the thin air had brought on euphoria. I heard myself laughing and saying rather stagily, 'Two minds with but a single thought.'

'Arre, don't try these mad tricks,' said the inspector in alarm. 'If the Chinia see you they will shoot you first and then ask who you are.'

'Sahib,' said one of the traders. 'On my mother's life, it is a mad thing to do.'

'Driver,' shouted Das, 'bring my movie-camera.' He cast the kind of glance a professional spy might have cast into the valley. 'While the mist gives us cover, we shall start. Lend us your field-glasses, inspector sahib.'

'Sir,' said the policeman, 'on my mother's and grandmother's lives, I should forbid you. What will come to me if you are killed or taken prisoner? I will lose my job!'

'Come on, Dom,' Das said to me.

So I took a final drink from the bottle, borrowed the inspector's field-glasses, turned my coat-collar up against the wind, and followed Das into the valley.

The slope was strewn with rocks, which afforded precarious handholds. We had to let ourselves down backward, like mountaineers, and I felt acutely conscious of the wind flapping my jacket, the field-glasses dangling round my neck, and the unseen Chinese probably even now gloating over us through their field-glasses, like uniformed Fu Manchus.

I reached the bottom of the slope a minute after Das. He did not hesitate, but set off at a brisk walk down the valley. The ground was rough and tussocky, the mist had thickened and it was impossibly cold. My limbs were like stalactites: lifting one became a creaking, breathless effort. Conversation was out of the question. I simply followed Das, and we were suddenly among trees.

Here there was a clean acid stench of wet earth and herbs. A bird or two shrieked upwards through the leaves, but otherwise everything was grave-silent. Our feet scuffing through the undergrowth sounded like a forest fire.

We walked for about twenty minutes, twice passing clearings where ashes remained in ersatz fireplaces made of heaped stones. Then Das stopped. We were both breathless. We sat down and I lit a cigarette. We talked in whispers.

'There don't seem to be any Chinese hereabouts.'

'Certainly we are not seeing any. But we must have come the best part of a mile. If we push on, we will be near the checkpost. If I can get a film of some troops without their seeing me, we shall have scooped the world.'

I no longer felt any apprehension. It seemed to me reasonable that Das should want to scoop the world. Apart from the difficulty of breathing properly in this rarefied air, I felt quite willing to go on.

'Those fireplaces, do you think they were made by the Chinese?' I was beginning to feel towards the Chinese now as I might toward the inhabitants of Troizen or Zimbabwe.

'Perhaps by the Chinese, perhaps by some muleteers. Let us get on.'

We stumbled through the trees. In the forest the mist seemed to be filtered away by the leaves, but overhead the sky was still clogged with grey. This unrewarding sky was our only window to the rest of the world for another twenty minutes, till we stumbled out of the forest on to a bare ridge, littered with chalky rock fragments, between two hillocks. Here we sat down again. I looked round through the field-glasses. We were a good way into the valley: the two great snowpeaks looked closer and the barren hummock of Nathu La surprisingly far. I put down the glasses and lit another cigarette. Das drummed his fingers on his knee.

'If we pushed on a little farther, we would get close enough to Chumbithan to take a film of the checkpost. Do you think that is a foolhardy plan?'

The clouds rifted: suddenly and fugitively the sun glared from a waste of blue. Idly I picked up the glasses and looked round. The sun caught them, and reflected light flashed on one of the neighbouring hillocks.

A moment later, there was an answering flash on the ridge where we sat. Das looked up in surprise. The flash was repeated. I looked through the glasses in the direction from which it came.

On the neighbouring hillock, clustered together, was a group of Chinese.

There were about twenty, stocky and tough-looking. Two were in a drab grey-green military uniform with peaked caps. These two were looking at us through field-glasses. The rest stood behind, sten guns and ammunition belts hung over their shoulders. They pointed at us, and were apparently discussing us among themselves.

I told Das. He said very coolly, 'Let us get back into the trees in case they open fire. I will take a film.' We moved back to the fringe of the forest. Das fitted the tele-lens on his camera. He knelt down, swivelling it for focus. I was unnerved, but not unpleasantly. I tried to analyse what I was feeling. I hoped to God that they wouldn't think Das's camera was a sten gun and open fire. I could feel my own heart beating very fast, and I kept on swallowing. But after the initial shock had worn off, I was able to calculate a few things. First, they could not be less than half a mile away. If our information about their weapons had been right, we were out of range. Second, we were going to have to hurry back, for they would certainly send men after us. Das's camera had begun to hum by my side. I put the glasses back on the Chinese. Half a dozen men and one of the officers were already moving downhill. The remaining officer continued to study us through his glasses.

Das's camera ceased to hum. He stood up and turned to me.

'A scoop. You noticed those men coming down the hill, hah? They are coming to get us. Therefore, I think we will have to run.'

He nodded toward Nathu La.

'Run straight back. We must not stop for anything. Mind the field-glasses, they belong to the inspector. Come on.'

Of the next half hour I remember very little. I am not a good runner anyway and in the thin clear air of the plateau I was worse than usual. The initial stumbling gallop through the forest rendered me breathless; then my ears filled with a buzzing that shut out all other sound; finally I developed a burning stitch in my left side. That is the physical memory, and there is one visual image: when we came to a small pebbled brook in the forest, I collapsed beside it and lay on my stomach watching the weeds waver slowly in the flow of the current, two long-legged water-flies, and a minnow; the moss was cool against my cheek. When I looked up Nathu La seemed far and unreachable. I was willing to stay where I was. Das's voice, breathless but imperative, brought me to a kind of reality.

'Come on. We are nearly there. Quickly!'

So flight began again. I reached Nathu La in a daze, a small iron needle in my side. We scrambled back up the slope and sat down heavily amongst a solicitous group of policeman, traders, and drivers.

'We were beginning to worry,' said the inspector.

'We also,' said Das, and managed a smile.

The mist had come on again, and there was no sign of the Chinese.

We lay on foam-rubber-textured lichen, getting our breath, and in my case helping it along with the remains of the brandy. One of the traders came and squatted beside us.

Das, sighing, heaved himself indefatigably up and reached for his notebook. 'This Indian who was killed. Tell me about him.'

'It was done by the Tibetans,' the trader said. 'They came to his shop in the afternoon, and stabbed him five times. Then they looted the shop, took the money from the cash-box, and left.'

'Tibetans?' Das said with professional disappointment. 'I thought you said Chinese.'

'The Chinese say they themselves are Tibetans who have come from Peking. But these real Tibetans were hired by the Chinia, sahib,' said the trader. 'They did it in the daytime and the bazaar was full of Chinia policemen, but they did not interfere, though he shouted for help.'

'Ha!' said Das, and scribbled enthusiastically. 'How do they treat you, these Chinese?'

'Sahib, in the daytime we cannot move more than two hundred yards from our houses without a permit. After nine o'clock we cannot leave our houses also. It is gaol life. Also they have taken the custom from our shops, and anything they buy they buy on credit, and never pay.'

'Why don't you complain to the Indian trade agent at Yatung? He is there to help you?'

'Sahib, what can he do? They pay no attention. And if we leave Tibet, they confiscate all our goods. Now we, today, were only allowed to bring our clothes and ten rupees from Yatung. They only have contempt for us Indians. Every Saturday in Yatung they have a clown show with four clowns, and one is Nehru.'

'Good, good!' said Das, scribbling a little more. 'Who are the other three?'

'Eisenhower sahib, Churchill sahib, and Khrushchev sahib.'

'Why Khrushchev?'

'They are very angry that Russia has not supported them over the border dispute.'

'What do they say about the border?'

'Sahib, the officers say one day soon they will be coming. At the checkpost at Chumbithan they told us to say that in Sikkim.'

'It may not be as easy as they think,' said the police officer dourly.

'The Chinia are strong,' the trader said.

'How do they treat the Tibetans?' I asked.

'Sahib, all the rich men they have put to building a military road from Shigatse. Also in Yatung two weeks ago they took all the young girls away. They do this to keep the men from running away; also the girls are useful in North Tibet, because they are settling many Chinia civilians there, and they have no women.'

'What about the rebels, the Khambas? Is there still any fighting?'

'With them also, they took their families and put them in gaol, until the husbands surrendered. Them they shot or put to work on the Shigatse road.'

He sat by us, sighing, gathering a little dust in his hand and sifting it away with the slow movements of a tired man. I noticed how jumpy all the traders were. They had lines under their eyes, and all of them had nervous twitchy gestures of the hand.

We sat there, thinking, drinking, and then the inspector said: 'Chhibar sahib is coming.'

Through the field-glasses a file of mules appeared ambling up the valley towards Nathu La. It was a relief. We squatted on the hummock watching them all the way up the valley till they had reached us.

Chhibar came first. He was a large man, rosy and powerful, wearing a fur hat and leather jacket. As his mule crested the ridge, we all shouted, rather raggedly, 'Welcome!' He smiled and waved a hand. After him came his wife, a most beautiful woman in a ballooning quilted jacket that made her look like a little tent, and three Tibetan nurses, each with one of the Chhibar offspring in her arms. They were followed by a baggage-train, the muleteers prodding the mules with goads and shouting the Tibetan version of Gittup: '*To to to to to to to*,' on a rising scale. 'Very picturesque,' said Das, going happily to work with his movie-camera. When he had finished, the Chhibar family dismounted, and Das handed his camera to the driver and fished for his notebook.

'How was your trip, Major Chhibar?'

'Fine, fine,' said Chhibar, smiling gently.

'What are these reports of your being hindered by Chinese troops on your journey?'

'Untrue,' Chhibar sighed.

'The Chinese were helpful?'

'To me, yes,' emphasizing the *me*.

'And to other Indians? Say, the traders?'

'Less helpful.'

'Would it be true to say that the traders are in fear of their lives?'

'Perhaps.' So large, so gentle, so like a wall blocking off undiplomatic questions.

'How many troops would you say there were in Tibet?'

'I can't say. It is a difficult question.'

'In Lhasa, then?'

'It is a difficult question. Ten thousand—fifteen thousand.'

'And between Lhasa and Nathu La?'

'It is a difficult question. Perhaps the same number again.'

'So there are between twenty and thirty thousand Chinese in the area between Lhasa and Nathu La?'

'I would say so, yes.'

'Hah!' said Das, but at this point Mrs Chhibar came up to introduce the children, and I became occupied in teaching one of the little girls how to whistle, and missed the rest.

Then the Chhibars left in the waiting jeep, and Nathu La was desolate again.

I went up to the hummock to get a last look at Tibet. All I saw was mist.

Coming Back

There was nothing to stay for, and in Gangtok I realized how dead the journey had become. Das did too, I think; we left for Kalimpong next day: city of spies. We ate in a Chinese restaurant where the radio played music from Radio Peking, and the waiters loitered about, rather obviously listening to the conversation of the customers. A day in Kalimpong, then to Bagdogra again, and back to Calcutta. I kept flying, going from Calcutta back to Bombay. So I had to say goodbye to Das: though I had only known him two weeks, goodbye was sad and strange.

But then all goodbyes are, even the ones in Bombay, with the servants lined up at the door with garlands and tears, Marilyn getting a fit of hiccups and my father pressing my air ticket into my hand like a deathbed relic.

I planned to go to Manila and Tashkent before returning to London but that is another story.

Flying is as strange as saying goodbye: to be above the world, swimming in the blue bird-sea with the clouds under, the air hostess bringing round the drinks, the passengers suddenly peaceful and beautiful people. Above the chaos of world folded into world, for ever and ever, world where nothing ends because nothing has ever truly and beautifully begun.

But landing in London is my beginning, my perpetual peaceful return to your hand in sleep at last made actual. I will bring back yaks to you in my head, and lamas; rice fields drying in the sun, the living and dying of a world half-the-world away. I can bring you nothing else, because all the rest comes from you.

It is raining in London. November: cold: I remember that I have not got my overcoat. But I put the thought of you on to warm me, and diligently I advance towards the Customs.

TAMAM SHUD

ALSO BY DOM MORAES IN SPEAKING TIGER

Where Some Things are Remembered: Profiles and Conversations

Dom Moraes was not only one of India's greatest poets, he was also an extraordinary journalist and essayist. He could capture effortlessly the essence of the people he met, and in every single profile in this sparkling collection he shows how it is done.

The Dalai Lama laughs with him and Mother Teresa teaches him a lesson in empathy. Moraes could make himself at home with Laloo Prasad Yadav, the man who invented the self-fulfilling controversy, and exchange writerly notes with Sunil Gangopadhyaya. He was Indira Gandhi's biographer—painting her in defeat, post Emergency, and in triumph, when she returned to power. He tried to fathom the mind of a mysterious 'super cop'—K.P.S. Gill—and also of Naxalites, dacoits and ganglords.

This collection is literary journalism at its finest—from an observer who saw people and places with the eye of a poet and wrote about them with the precision of a surgeon.

Price: ₹499; Page extent: 208; ISBN: 978-93-88326-68-1

ALSO BY DOM MORAES IN SPEAKING TIGER

Under Something of A Cloud: Selected Travel Writing

Under Something of a Cloud spans a lifetime of Dom Moraes' work to select the very best of his travel writing. Featured in this volume is a vividly recollected childhood tour of Sri Lanka, Southeast Asia and Australia with his father, Frank Moraes, and his mother, Beryl, who was then rapidly sliding into madness; a darkly comic account of a trip to the Sikkim-Tibet border, amidst rumours that the Chinese would soon attack India; and a thrilling adventure among the Dani tribe in Indonesia who, at that time, were reputed to be cannibals.

Also included here are Moraes' sojourns among dacoits in the Chambal valley, one of whom, Lacchi, he helped spring from police custody; an evocative account of a 'madai', a fair where the Maria tribals of Madhya Pradesh gathered to barter goods and find life partners; and encounters with women victims in Ahmedabad, soon after the riots in 2002, which left him shattered.

With a keen sense for atmosphere, colour, understated wit and unfailing empathy for the underdog, Dom Moraes brings to life people and places like few other writers anywhere can. Not only will fans of the author love *Under Something of a Cloud*, it will also appeal to readers of world-class travel writing and connoisseurs of timeless prose.

Price: ₹599; Page extent: 236; ISBN: 978-93-88326-65-0